Basic River Canoeing

Robert E. McNair
Matty L. McNair
Paul A. Landry

American Camping Association

**This Book
Is Dedicated to
All Rivers Wild and Free**

Table of Contents

FOREWORD

From its small beginnings, river canoeing in the United States has grown enormously and evolved along many channels. New equipment, materials, and techniques have advanced the capabilities of boaters tremendously. Racing and cruising on all levels of rivers in the U.S. are enjoyed by large numbers of people from all over the country. River guidebooks, racing manuals and books on advanced techniques have been published in large numbers. However, in spite of all this, there is still a critical need for clear, understandable instruction for beginners and novice boaters to provide a safe and enjoyable introduction to the sport. The original *Basic River Canoeing* served this purpose well in the past and has now been extensively revised and brought up-to-date by Bob McNair (the original author) and Paul and Matty McNair Landry (son-in-law and daughter of Bob).

The roots of this book reach back into the post World War II era when a group of outdoor enthusiasts from the Buck Ridge Ski Club in the Philadelphia area began teaching themselves whitewater canoeing, a new sport in the U.S. There were other scattered groups in Colorado and New England also learning to paddle and enjoy the fast flowing streams, but no organized means existed for others outside these groups to learn the basics. To help other clubs and groups get safely started on the rivers, Buck Ridge members developed "Red Ridge College." This weekend course, offered to leaders of outdoor clubs, attracted students from all over the Eastern United States and did much to spread safe river canoeing. The course material developed for Red Ridge was later combined and edited by Bob McNair, one of the pioneers in the sport in America. This produced the book *Basic River Canoeing*, which was originally published in 1968 by Buck Ridge. It sold out quickly. Subsequently, the American Camping Association assumed the publication with several additional printings preceding this new edition.

Bob, Paul, and Matty have rewritten the original book to incorporate new and up-to-date knowledge and techniques. The authors have produced an excellent primer for basic boaters. I believe this to be an excellent and enjoyable introduction for beginners as well as a valuable guide for intermediate paddlers who have had no formal training. Better to make mistakes on the Hypothetical River than to take a chilly dip in your local stream. Matty and Paul bring extensive experience and training in running rivers and outdoor education to this revision.

Bob, a retired research engineer for Westinghouse Corporation, now divides his time between his home in Swarthmore, Pennsylvania, and the McNair family farm in Madison, New Hampshire. Besides canoeing he has strong interests in Scottish dancing, bicycling (collecting and riding both modern and antique bicycles), and collecting antique carriages and sleighs. He is a founding member of the Buck Ridge Ski Club, a co-founder of the American Whitewater Affiliation, and one of the organizers of the Brandywine Canoe Slalom, the first in the U.S. Bob was the first National Slalom chairman for the American Canoe Association and received the esteemed Michelob Schooner Award from the United States Coast Guard for his contributions to boating safety. Bob has truly been one of the pioneers in whitewater canoeing in the U.S. and in promoting knowledge, skill and safety in the sport.

Matty grew up paddling, biking, and hiking with her father, Bob, and the rest of the McNair family. She has a degree in Outdoor Experential Learning from Beacon College and has been an outdoor instructor for the Outdoor Learning Center at Bemidji State College in Minnesota. She has taught ski mountaineering, rock climbing, and winter camping as well as wilderness canoeing.

Paul, born in northern Ontario, attended the University of Western Ontario and Northern Ontario College and has traveled in Europe and the Middle East. He spent two seasons on the flatwater marathon canoe racing circuit in Ontario.

Both Paul and Matty have developed, directed, and instructed whitewater and wilderness canoe courses for Hurricane Island and Canadian Outward Bound schools. Their river experience includes the Grand Canyon of the Colorado and extended wilderness river trips on the Missinaibi and other rivers leading to Hudson Bay. They have paddled widely on Eastern and Western rivers and have raced in whitewater slalom competition.

Their first child, Eric, was born recently and can probably look forward to his first canoeing experience in the near future.

MARK S. FAWCETT

(Mark S. Fawcett learned whitewater canoeing with Buck Ridge Ski Club after an early interest in canoeing developed from trips as a teenager in the Boundary Waters Canoe Area in the 1950s. He holds a number of championships in slalom, wildwater world class, and is a whitewater instructor trainer for the American Canoe Association.)

Preface

Are you interested in taking up the sport of whitewater canoeing, further developing your paddling skills, or involved in teaching canoeing? If you are, then this book is for you. It is written for people like you who wish to learn and improve their whitewater canoeing skills.

The emphasis of *Basic River Canoeing* is to teach you the art of safely paddling a canoe through whitewater with skill, finesse, and style. This book explains the techniques of whitewater canoeing, with concise instructions and clear illustrations, for an enjoyable and safe introduction to the sport. Oriented to the open two-person canoe, the material presented in this book (except for specific strokes) also is applicable to solo paddling and closed canoes.

For simplicity, the authors have artifically divided the first part of this book into equipment, strokes, water reading, river maneuvers, and rescues. In the later chapters, the authors have tried to blend this knowledge back together to give a complete concept of how these skills are used to play the river, take on the challenges of a slalom, or venture down a wilderness river. The last chapter is dedicated to all those who, like the authors, enjoy teaching whitewater canoeing.

Hopefully, this book will be only a beginning. You are encouraged to search the book shelves for other excellent whitewater books and to join paddling clubs and attend whitewater schools to refine skills and broaden knowledge. Above all, this book is intended to give a solid understanding of basic whitewater canoeing so you can develop skills and experience to safely enjoy the fast-flowing rivers of our country.

Robert, Matty and Paul

Chapter I

Equipment and Clothing

You owe it to yourself to get the very best equipment. Quality equipment will give you good performance, the greatest safety, and the most pleasure. Personal likes and dislikes in equipment and clothing vary considerably so buy what is best for you. "Best" does not necessarily mean the most expensive. Sometimes you will choose to pay a high price because this equipment will be more economical in the long run. At other times, you can adapt some old gear to be just exactly right for your canoeing needs. Consider first obtaining the right design and material; then note the price. The best canoe is the one that provides the fewest compromises to suit your needs: weight versus strength, speed versus maneuverability, etc. It may be better for you to buy a secondhand canoe or a factory second canoe, with blemishes that do not affect performance, than to buy a brand new one of inferior design, material, or workmanship. Over many years of paddling the initial cost of equipment will become insignificant.

A CANOE FOR YOU

The first great material change came about one hundred years ago when birch bark gave way to cedar strip canoes covered with canvas. These canoes are still built today, both commercially and by talented individuals. They are beautiful for quiet waters and have a long life if stored properly, maintained conscientiously, and used with care.

Aluminum canoes, introduced by Grumman after World War II, opened a new era of canoeing. Aluminum is virtually maintenance-free, very durable, and can take tremendous abuse. Therefore, these canoes are often used by institutions and rental outfits. On the other hand, aluminum is hard to patch, noisy, cold, aesthetically ugly, and tends to "grab" rocks. Most aluminum canoes have conservative lines, designed for the average recreational paddler. If you decide on an aluminum boat, you will want a keel-less or shoe-keel canoe reinforced with extra ribs.

Fiberglass appeared as a canoe material around 1955. Today almost all whitewater and flatwater racing boats are made of fiberglass. By fiberglass we mean fibers of glass which are saturated with a liquid resin. The most common types of cloth include: E-glass, S-glass, nylon and Dupont's Kevlar® . Types of resin include polyester, vinylester, and epoxy. Quality depends largely on the type and combination of materials used and the method by which it is layed-up. Hand lay-ups, in which each individual sheet

1

of cloth is placed in the mold and soaked with resin, is more expensive and stronger than a gun-sprayed boat in which cloth and resin are sprayed onto a mold.

Kevlar is an amazing cloth that is used to build the strongest and lightest canoes. Since the cloth is more expensive than regular glass, you will seldom find an all Kevlar boat. Most manufacturers will use various ratios of Kevlar and glass cloth in their lay-ups. They might use one layer of Kevlar with four of E-glass or three of Kevlar with two of S-glass. When buying a Kevlar boat ask about the lay-up.

Fiberglass owes its popularity to its ease in being inexpensively molded into innovative and competitive designs. Fiberglass canoes are easy to repair and can be built in your backyard or through a club. They do, however, lack the abrasion and impact resistance of aluminum and ABS boats.

Royalex® /ABS (Acrylonitrile-Butadiene-Styrene) is a rubber product from Uniroyal. It is delivered to canoe manufacturers in laminated sheets, with the hard rubber exteriors sandwiching a foam core. Old Town was the first company to heat and vacuum mold these sheets into various hull designs. Today many boat manufacturers order special, slightly different ABS laminates from Uniroyal and trim the boats in wood, plastic or aluminum. ABS boat manufacturers claim that the foam sandwich construction provides flotation, but be ready to have your canoe disappear out of sight in big whitewater. You would be wise to add extra flotation if the company has not supplied it already. Also, bow and stern skid or abrasion plates will prolong the life of your canoe.

ABS is tough, flexible, and requires little maintenance. It is the slipperiest of all canoe materials and will slide over rocks without a sound. But the material on the inside is just as slippery as the outside, making knee straps a must. Many ABS canoes currently do not have a sharp entry line; they have a floppy bottom when not loaded and are difficult to repair if torn. They are generally heavier and more expensive than aluminum and fiberglass canoes.

DIFFERENT SHAPES

When choosing a canoe, the hull shape and design are more important than materials and weight. The key factors to examine are the rocker (keel-line curvature from bow to stern) and the hull cross-section. In evaluating a canoe, try to strike a balance that will fit your style of paddling.

For simplicity, we have condensed designs into three categories: downriver, recreational, and slalom. At one end of the spectrum is the downriver canoe, designed for straight-as-an-arrow speed. At the other extreme is the slalom canoe which spins on a wave like a dancer. Both of these high performance, specialized boats are designed for advanced paddlers and have limited versatility. If you plan to do long wilderness canoe trips you will want to choose a canoe between a downriver and recreational model. If you are more interested in playing the rapids, choose a design between a recreational and a slalom canoe.

Downriver

The downriver canoe has a straight keel line (no rocker) and a V-shaped hull. These boats are very fast and easy to keep on a straight course. The V bottom slices through the water like a knife and adds rigidity to the hull. Initially, these boats will feel tippy, but they become more stable with speed. The lack of rocker makes this boat difficult to turn; though in whitewater, current differentials may catch the straight-keel-line and turn you against your wish. These designs are high performance flatwater and downriver racing boats. Lengths vary between sixteen and eighteen and a half feet.

Recreational

Today most manufacturers are selling boats with moderate rocker and a flat bottom. This middle-of-the-line canoe well suits the average recreational paddler. For long wilderness trips a seventeen foot canoe with thirteen to fifteen inches depth will be adequate for you and your gear. A fifteen to sixteen foot canoe with slightly more rocker is ideal for one- or two-day runs on narrow, rocky rivers. Moderate rocker makes this craft more maneuverable and much easier to turn while the flat bottom is more stable in calm water.

Slalom

The slalom canoe is designed with extreme rocker to enable it to spin quickly. Their round bottoms make them easy to lean but frustratingly tippy for beginners. About sixteen feet long, these high performance canoes are most often seen at slalom races. Experienced paddlers will find this responsive boat a joy to paddle in whitewater. It would be, however, a poor choice for a long wilderness trip as you will waste much energy keeping it on a straight course.

PADDLES

Paddles have come a long way from the old standard one-piece solid wood. A good paddle is a lifelong friend, so you need something that will be dependable, strong, and well balanced. Wood paddles range from poor to excellent, depending on the type and quality of wood and workmanship. One-piece spruce paddles are fine for lakes but not strong enough for whitewater. Ash, cherry, and maple are stronger. They also are heavier. The ideal wood paddle is a laminate combining different woods for strength and lightness. A laminated paddle is expensive, but if it is cared for it will last many years. To protect the blade from fraying or splitting, a metal or fiberglass tip can be added (see Appendix I).

Fiberglass paddles with aluminum shafts are the toughest and the favorite for running rocky rivers. They are durable and need little maintenance but lack the lively spring of wood. A good fiberglass paddle will cost about as much or more than a good wood laminated paddle.

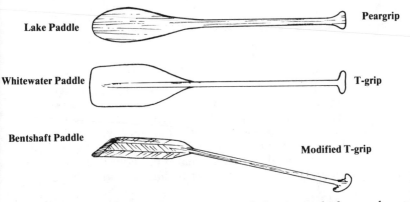

Lake Paddle   **Peargrip**

Whitewater Paddle   **T-grip**

Bentshaft Paddle   **Modified T-grip**

Paddles made with hard plastic blades and aluminum shafts are also good for whitewater, although with abuse the blades do crack. They are relatively inexpensive and are good for institutional use.

Paddle length, blade width or handle shape depends mostly on your physique and personal preference. Try as many different types of paddles as you can before buying one. Here are some guidelines to consider: Standard length is up to your chin or nose. More and more whitewater paddlers prefer shorter paddles. Blade width should range from between six to eight inches. The wider the blade the more water it can pull; but if it is too wide for your body build, you will not be able to keep a fast tempo, and you will tire more quickly. A T-grip handle offers excellent blade control and minimizes the chances of the paddle being snatched out of your hands.

Bent-shaft paddles made their appearance a number of years ago on the flatwater racing circuit. They are now being used for downriver races and sometimes for general touring. The angle at the throat (anywhere from five to fifteen degrees) gives you a more efficient and powerful stroke. They are not used in slalom paddling where both sides of the blade are needed.

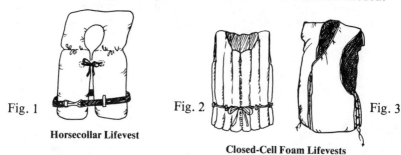

Fig. 1   Fig. 2   Fig. 3

Horsecollar Lifevest

Closed-Cell Foam Lifevests

LIFEVESTS

Anyone who ventures out in whitewater without wearing an adequate lifevest does not quite understand the force of moving water. When choosing a lifevest do not compromise on quality. Be sure to buy a Coast Guard approved lifevest that will match your own buoyancy requirements. Get one that allows paddling freedom and fits comfortably so that you will not resent wearing it all day.

The old standard horseshoe collar keeps your head out of the water but is uncomfortable and will lose buoyancy if the plastic compartments, filled with kapok, are punctured (Fig. 1). The panel style and vertical ribbed models of closed-cell foam with zippers up the front are, by far, the best choices (Figs. 2 & 3). The added flotation around the back is necessary in whitewater and will protect your back from rocks during a swim through rapids.

HELMETS

Helmets are recommended for decked canoes and kayaks. When a covered boat goes over, you remain in it to try and roll it back up. Therefore, you need to protect your head from rocks. In an open canoe the

Whitewater Helmet

Hockey Helmet

paddler leaves the boat as it capsizes and, hopefully, the head remains above water. Many open canoe paddlers wear helmets in rocky rivers with powerful currents and in slaloms where swinging gates can injure them. If you value your brain cells, wear a brain bucket. Although there are some good whitewater helmets, beware of lightweight helmets with thin plastic shells and little energy absorbing liners which do not offer adequate protection. Hockey helmets are a good alternative.

CANOE RIGGING

Knee straps are invaluable! They give you a firm hold on the canoe to maintain leans and keep you from sliding around the bottom of your boat while your hands are busy with the paddle. The added control will reduce spills. When you do capsize, the straps should fall free as soon as you release outward pressure. Once you have tried them you will be impressed with the confidence the straps give you, and you will never want to paddle whitewater again without them.

To install straps in an aluminum canoe, cut strips one-inch wide by six inches long from a sheet of hardened aluminum of the kind that is supplied for patching canoes. Two are needed for each end of the canoe. Bend them up in the center to allow a one-inch strap to pass under. The strap anchor should be positioned three inches on either side of the keel and about four inches back from the front of your knees when kneeling. Drill four holes through the strips and bottom of canoe and rivet together. A single nylon strap about eight feet long with a strong buckle is then laced through the strips and back to the seat. On some canoes you will need to cut holes through the seats a few inches from the sides to allow for the strap.

For fiberglass and ABS canoes you can buy "D-ring neoprene patches" and glue them into the bottom with contact cement. If you own a fiberglass

Neoprene Rafters "D" Rings

Homemade Ring for Fiberglass Boats

boat, there is another option. Make a loop at the center of a twelve-inch length of rope, fray both ends and saturate with resin to the bottom of the canoe. Cover this with a few round patches of cloth and resin. If your canoe has no keel you can use one knee strap anchor, centering it no more than four inches back from your knees.

To protect the knees, fashion knee pads from closed-cell foam. With contact cement, glue the pads into the canoe where your knees will rest.

Painters, secured to each end of the canoe, are essential for rescuing a capsized boat in a rapid, lining around a tricky section of river, or tying your canoe at lunch. Ten to fifteen feet is adequate for recreational whitewater. On long wilderness trips twenty-five-foot painters,

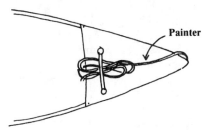

for lining, will come in handy. Choose a bright colored rope that floats. A diameter of three-eighths inch is an overkill on strength but will save your hands from getting rope burn when rescuing a swamped canoe. It is best to coil your bow and stern painters and secure them to your deck with shock cord or velcro. They will be out of the way during a capsize or portage.

RIGGING YOUR CANOE

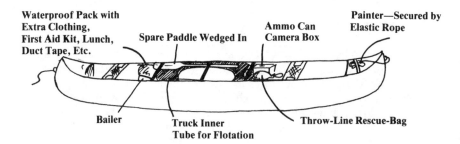

Flotation supplied with your canoe is barely enough to float it with gunwales above the surface. Adding extra flotation is a must for whitewater. The flotation added to your canoe will displace the water that would otherwise make it an unwieldy elephant in the event of an upset. Flotation also makes your swamped canoe ride higher through the waves and less likely to catch and crumple around rocks. Styrofoam blocks or large inflatable bags are usually available at canoe stores. A big truck inner tube inflated in your boat will provide as much flotation at a much cheaper price.

Splash Covers will allow you to run rapids that would otherwise swamp an open canoe. They also help keep you dry and warmer on rainy, cold days. But they certainly do not make you a better paddler! The few companies that make them limit production to the more popular canoes. If you are ambitious, you can make a splash cover out of durable waterproof material and attach it to your canoe with snaps and/or two-inch wide velcro.

Bailers are useful to scoop out water sloshing around the bottom of your canoe while you are resting in an eddy. Make them by cutting the bottom off of one-gallon plastic milk jugs or bleach bottles. Do not forget to tie them in.

Carrying Yokes make carrying a canoe more comfortable. They help put the weight of the canoe directly over your shoulders and

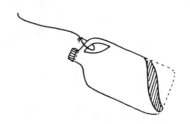

Please—Don't Litter the River with Your Bailers!

provide padding. An alternative, for short carries, is to carry the canoe by the center thwart padded by a heavy sweater or lifevest.

CLOTHING

Clothing fashion for canoeing ranges from old running shoes and bathing suits to flashy paddling jackets and wet suits (Fig. 4). The appropriate choice should be dictated by safety, function, comfort, and durability. Consider whether you will need protection from the sun, wind, rain, or cold. What is the temperature of the water? To allow for errors in your expectations, bring extra clothes either with you on the river or to change into later.

WATERPROOFING

According to Murphy's law, if your extra clothes, lunch, and camera are not waterproofed and secured, your canoe will turn over! Waterproof river bags can be found at canoe stores or ordered through rafting and paddling suppliers. (See advertisements in whitewater magazines.) A cheaper option is to line your day pack with a heavy plastic bag, double bag everything, and tie it tightly. Commercially made waterproof camera bags are available, but can puncture and are not always convenient. Small ammunition boxes, sold at Army-Navy stores, are great for cameras, sunglasses, and guide books.

When packing your gear for a day of frolicking in the rapids or an overnight trip, a couple of river bags or packs are better than a number of small items. Be sure everything is tied in with quick release knots or snap rings as wet knots can be difficult in rescue operations.

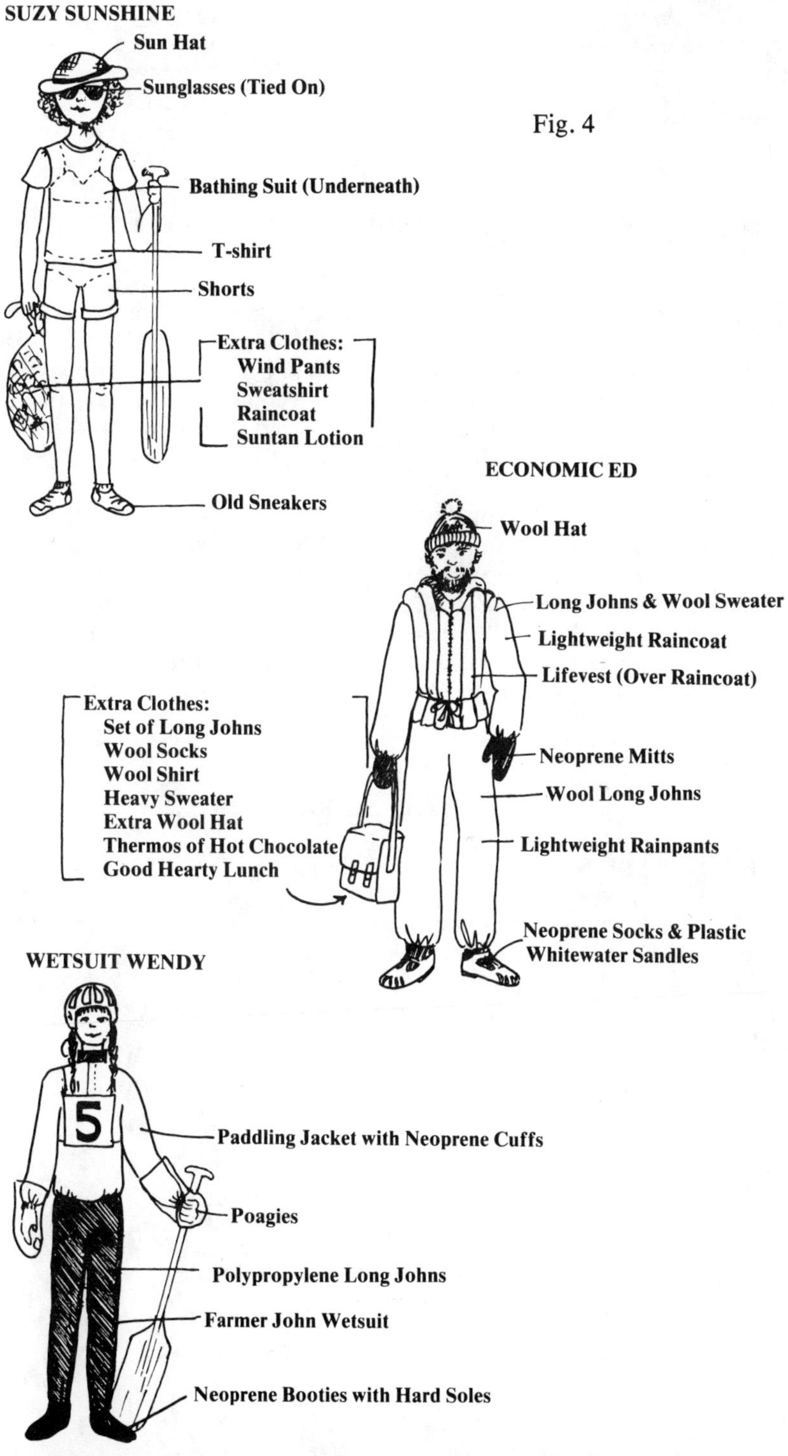

SUZY SUNSHINE
- Sun Hat
- Sunglasses (Tied On)
- Bathing Suit (Underneath)
- T-shirt
- Shorts
- Extra Clothes:
  - Wind Pants
  - Sweatshirt
  - Raincoat
  - Suntan Lotion
- Old Sneakers

Fig. 4

ECONOMIC ED
- Wool Hat
- Long Johns & Wool Sweater
- Lightweight Raincoat
- Lifevest (Over Raincoat)
- Neoprene Mitts
- Wool Long Johns
- Lightweight Rainpants
- Neoprene Socks & Plastic Whitewater Sandles

Extra Clothes:
- Set of Long Johns
- Wool Socks
- Wool Shirt
- Heavy Sweater
- Extra Wool Hat
- Thermos of Hot Chocolate
- Good Hearty Lunch

WETSUIT WENDY
- 5
- Paddling Jacket with Neoprene Cuffs
- Poagies
- Polypropylene Long Johns
- Farmer John Wetsuit
- Neoprene Booties with Hard Soles

Chapter 2

Making Your Paddle Strokes More Effective

Y ou may be clever at reading whitewater and quick in deciding on a good river strategy, but there is only one way you can implement your plan—using your paddle and using it effectively. You do not have to be terribly strong; you just have to be fast and accurate with a technique that makes the most of your strength. Your paddle must fly into action instantly and by habit execute the one best stroke for that situation. This will come with practice and experience.

This chapter will help you analyze and develop precision strokes. To understand the simple dynamics of strokes, they have been divided into perfect strokes and combination strokes. Perfect strokes are those that only move you forward, backward, right, or left. They are the forward, back, draw and pry strokes. All other strokes are combination strokes that combine two or more aspects of perfect strokes and/or braces. For example, a reverse sweep done in the stern is a combination of a pry and back stroke motion.

Perfect Strokes

THE FORWARD STROKE

The forward stroke comes almost naturally, but a few key points need to be stressed to help you paddle all day without tiring.

Keep the paddle straight up and down and not diagonally across your chest (Fig. 1). This gives a straight stroke parallel to the keel and allows you to throw your weight into the stroke for maximum drive.

Fig. 1

Like This　　　　　**Not Like This**

Make your back and shoulders do most of the work to ease the burden on your arms. The power in the stroke comes from the top arm driving and less from the bottom arm pulling. It is a good exercise to paddle with both arms straight while learning to use your back and shoulder muscles.

Feather your paddle on the recovery (rotating top hand thumb forward) so that the blade returns parallel to the water. Feathering allows the paddle to reduce wind resistance and by swinging low and wide eliminates the need to lift your paddle high. (Watch your lower arm to insure that it does not bend and lift.) After the power drive, learn to relax through the recovery.

Use a short, quick stroke. The power in the forward stroke is most effective during the paddle's vertical travel and decreases after it passes your hips. This is the stroke used by whitewater paddlers and flatwater racers because it is more efficient, less tiring, and corrections can be incorporated more quickly.

THE BACK STROKE

This is the stroke for backing out of trouble; it is the stroke to give you more time to think when you can go neither right nor left, and the prospect ahead is disturbing. It is also the stroke to ease the blow when all else has failed. Too often people use the forward stroke when they panic, which only drives the canoe faster toward catastrophe.

Fig. 2

COMPOUND BACK STROKE

Pull→

Flip

→ Push

Reach Back and Pull **Flip Paddle Over** **Finish with Back Stroke**

The back stroke is similar to the forward stroke done in reverse. It is very important to stroke on a line parallel to the keel with a vertical paddle (Fig. 1). Otherwise you will spin your canoe.

To hold a straight course when moving backward, the bow person must learn to finish the back stroke with a reverse 'J' or a quick pry off the bow.

The "compound back stroke" is a more powerful and effective means to propel your canoe backward. Rotate your body so you can reach way back to pull water. When the paddle reaches your hip, flip the blade and finish with a back stroke (Fig. 2). The sequence may seem difficult at first, but with practice it will flow smoothly. Practice backing on flatwater until you have developed a powerful back stroke and can keep the canoe on a straight course. Remember to keep the stroke on a line parallel to the keel.

THE DRAW

The draw stroke pulls the end of the canoe toward your paddle. Keeping the paddle nearly vertical, reach far out to your side and dig the paddle deep into the water. Quickly pull the water to the canoe. To gain maximum turning efficiency, the stroke should be done furthest from the turning fulcrum with the bow person's

Draw Stroke

stroke finishing next to the knee and the stern person's stroke at the hip. For a fast recovery, drop the top of the paddle away from you and with a quick twist (rotating top hand thumb away from body) slice the blade out of the water.

Contrary to one's expectation, the draw stroke has a righting effect on the canoe. The force on the paddle is well below the surface while the water drag on the canoe is at the surface. With your knees properly holding the canoe, as soon as the power is applied the canoe will indeed tip away from the paddling side. This allows you to lean far out, putting power into your stroke without tipping over. The bracing force stops when you stop pulling, so you must recover quickly.

THE PRY

The pry is the counterpart to the draw, pushing the canoe away from your paddle. Start by slicing your paddle under your canoe. To get the blade way under, rotate your shoulders and stretch your top arm far out over the side of the canoe. Now twist the paddle so the blade is parallel to the keel (turning top hand's thumb back). Pull your top arm so that the paddle shaft pries off the bilge of the canoe. When your paddle is just beyond the vertical—stop. Use an underwater recovery (twisting top hand's thumb away from body) to slice your paddle back under the canoe.

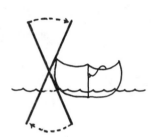

Pry Stroke

For complete mastery of this difficult but powerful stroke, understanding some common faults may help. If the top hand does not start way out over the water the stroke will be too short and ineffective.

If you try to lengthen the stroke by pulling across your chest, the paddle will lift water and rock your canoe by pushing down on the gunwale. Dropping the paddle deeper in the water will give you a longer stroke. This necessitates sliding your bottom hand up the shaft to avoid being pinched.

THE CROSSDRAW

Another counterpart to the draw for the bow person is the crossdraw. Without changing your hand position, swing the paddle over the bow to your off side. The paddle should be almost parallel to the water with the top hand

Cross Draw

near the gunwale and the blade pointed forward. Lean forward, and with your upper body, pull the water to the bow of the canoe. Lift the blade out of the water to reach out for another stroke.

When to use the crossdraw is still controversial among many canoeists. An easy stroke to learn, it is effective in shallow water, because the horizontal blade gives more surface area to pull water. Also, when coming in and out of eddies, the crossdraw helps the bow person lean into the turn. If you are using crossdraws to make continuous corrections, the paddle spends too much time out of the water. Furthermore, it is an isolated stroke and cannot be blended into the strokes that go before and after it. Unexpected weight shifts during crossdraws often result in spills.

Choosing between a pry and a crossdraw is a matter of personal style, river situations, and previous training. Learn them both and use where appropriate.

Combination Strokes

SWEEPS

Sweeps are used in both the bow and the stern to turn the canoe. Though not as powerful as the pry, they offer more stability. A forward sweep in the bow pushes the front of the canoe away from your paddle (combining a pry and forward motion). Start your stroke as far forward as you can reach; with the paddle close to the canoe, push the water in a long arc away from the bow until the paddle is perpendicular to the boat (Fig. 3).

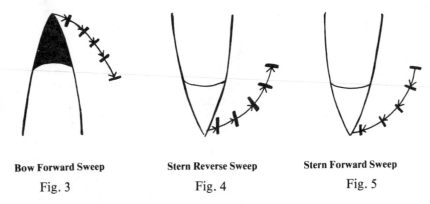

Bow Forward Sweep

Fig. 3

Stern Reverse Sweep

Fig. 4

Stern Forward Sweep

Fig. 5

While the bow person is doing a forward sweep, the stern person is often matching it with a reverse sweep. This stroke pushes the stern away from your paddle (combining a pry and backward motion). Start your stroke as far back as you can reach and as close to the stern as possible. Push the water in a long arc away from the stern until the paddle is perpendicular to the canoe. Be careful not to revert to a back stroke in an attempt to lean on your paddle. The reverse sweep is a good stroke to use in combination with a low brace when turning in or out of an eddy (Fig. 4).

The forward sweep used in the stern pulls the back of the canoe toward your paddle (combining a draw and forward motion). Extend your paddle so it is perpendicular to the canoe and sweep the water in a long arc pulling in toward the stern. This stroke is used to come in and out of eddies on your off side or as a correction stroke to keep the canoe on a straight course (Fig. 5).

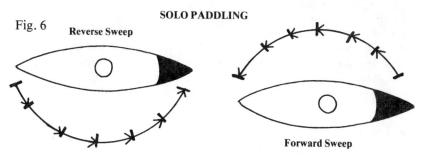

SOLO PADDLING

Fig. 6

Reverse Sweep

Forward Sweep

In perfecting your sweeps (both forward and reverse), keep your top hand low over the water so the paddle is more horizontal than vertical. The most important part of these strokes is the twelve inches closest to the canoe while the paddle is pushing or pulling water. To return for another stroke, feather your blade the same as you do in a forward stroke.

The sweep strokes that were described above are quarter sweeps. If you are paddling solo, you will need to do half sweeps, since you are both the bow and the stern person (Fig. 6).

'J' STROKES

The 'J' stroke is a combination stroke in which the forward stroke is finished with a pry motion. This helps the stern person keep the canoe tracking on a straight line, eliminating any need to change paddling sides. It is an important stroke to master since it gives a quick correction without ruddering, which interrupts the paddling tempo and brakes your gliding momentum.

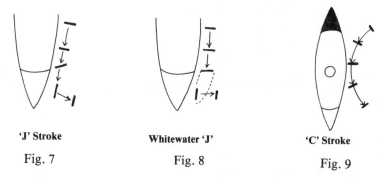

'J' Stroke

Fig. 7

Whitewater 'J'

Fig. 8

'C' Stroke

Fig. 9

To perfect the conventional 'J' stroke, turn the thumb of the top hand down ninety degrees (thumb should point to the water) at the end of each stroke, and give a small outward hook with your lower hand to provide the corrective push-away force. Both wrists should be cocked forward (Fig. 7).

A common fault is that the thumb is not turned down far enough. You must turn the paddle blade perpendicular to the surface of the water or the hook lifts water instead of pushing. Another common problem is starting the hook too far away from the canoe. This is often caused by the paddle being across the chest and not vertical.

A more powerful version of this stroke is what is called a whitewater 'J' stroke. It is a combination of the forward stroke finished with a quick pry. Here, at the end of the forward stroke, the thumb of the top hand is turned back and the paddle is pried off the stern of the canoe with a quick snap (Fig. 8).

'C' STROKE

The 'C' stroke used in solo canoeing is a combination of a draw, forward stroke, and pry motion as it follows the outline of the letter 'C'. The key points are to reach way forward with a combination forward and draw stroke and finish way behind with a 'J' stroke. Beginning solo paddlers will find themselves constantly tempted to change sides because mastery of the 'C' stroke seems so elusive (Fig. 9).

THE LOW BRACE

Braces are very important in white-water canoeing. Not only do we use our paddle to propel the canoe in any direction, but also to lean it into turns, to save an impending upset and even to roll a decked canoe from an upside down position.

Low Brace

To do a low brace, slap your paddle flat on the water, dropping both hands in the water and push off the surface with a quick downward thrust. To achieve a more powerful bracing and righting force pull up with the top hand while punching down with the lower hand.

The low brace is used by both bow and stern paddlers to save the canoe from turning over. The stern person can also combine a low brace with a reverse sweep when entering or leaving an eddy when the lean of the canoe is on the stern person's paddling side.

THE HIGH BRACE

Sometimes you need a brace, a draw, and a canoe lean all at once. This is particularly true when it is the bow person's lean and draw on entering or leaving an eddy. The high brace fulfills this combination of strokes. When

High Brace

coming into an eddy, the bow paddler reaches forward to plant the paddle deep in the still eddy water. Holding your paddle in a vertical position, you will feel a strong pull on your paddle which will give you a righting force on which to lean the canoe. When leaving the eddy, do a high brace by reaching out and digging your paddle into the fast current and lean into the turn. Finish with a draw and a forward stroke.

PUTTING IT ALL TOGETHER

Now that you have learned strokes to give you any desired effect from a single side, there is no need to waste precious time waving your paddle in the air from side to side. Your canoe will be much more stable when both of you are paddling on opposite sides, always ready to do a brace if the need arises. Change sides periodically; but do it together and not to correct incompetent steering. Develop equal skills on both your left and right sides to employ both sets of muscles. Try switching bow and stern positions, too. The more versatile you become the better paddler you will be.

Paddling in unison provides more stability, is more efficient, and keeps high performance canoes tracking straighter. The bow person usually sets the pace. When not paddling, hold your paddle in a ready position, keeping it vertical in the water about a foot away from the side of the canoe. From this position you are ready to perform any stroke in split seconds.

Fine-tune your stroke by varying the paddle depth and the blade angle to the current. For example, most people doing a high brace when leaving an eddy will have their blade parallel to the keel of the canoe. For a more powerful turning stroke, cock your wrists and twist your paddle so the current hits your blade at ninety degrees.

In whitewater the strokes should come quickly, flawlessly, and automatically while your mind is reading water and formulating strategy. With time you will learn to flow smoothly from one stroke to the next or to combine strokes to give two effects at once. With experience will come finesse and style. Adjust your knee straps, put your faith in your paddle, your paddle in the water, and off you go.

Chapter 3

The Art of Reading Fast Water

There is beauty in fast water. The patterns and colors are a painting and the sounds a symphony. These matters you must discover for yourself. This chapter will focus on the skill of interpreting fast water to help you see rocks where none are visible and see clear passages where only chaos greets the untrained eye.

Whitewater may look like chaos to the inexperienced eye.

Moving water is tremendously powerful. Coasting down a rapid at six miles an hour may seem tame, but do not be deceived! Before you conduct an expensive test let us analyze a situation. Suppose your canoe is pinned on a rock perpendicular to the current. The force of the water on the canoe is the area the canoe presents to the water times the water velocity squared times 2.8. (This presumes a drag coefficient of 1.) Since the current is six miles an hour, the force on your sixteen-foot canoe is about $16 \times 2 \times 6^2 \times 2.8 = 3225$ pounds! Suppose the water is only up to your thighs and you try to stand. The above formula gives a 300-pound force on your legs. Perhaps now you will want the water to work for you and not against you.

CURRENT DIFFERENTIALS

"Still waters run deep" and, conversely, fast waters run shallow. These are corollaries of a fundamental bit of common sense. Consider two places on the same river: where the river is deep and wide, the current is slow; where it is shallow and narrow, the current must run faster to pass the same volume of water. Once you have the feel of a stream on a particular day, you can deduce the depth from observation of width and velocity.

If it is slow and narrow, it must be deep.

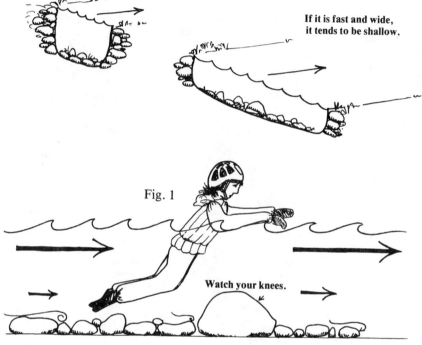

If it is fast and wide, it tends to be shallow.

Fig. 1

Watch your knees.

Current flows faster on the surface.

The water velocity is not constant all across the river. Water flows fastest on the surface in midstream. Friction slows the water along the bottom and along the shores. This is why you must back ashore when landing or the current differential will spin your canoe around. When you swim a rapid on your back with your feet downstream, you must keep your feet at the surface or the current differential will tumble you and have you going head first (Fig. 1).

Current direction is generally parallel to the banks. The most common exception is in sharp bends where the fast surface water flows diagonally to the outside of the bend. Often there are large waves or fallen trees on the outside, and inexperienced paddlers are swept into them to their surprise and dismay. Although their canoe is parallel to the banks, it is broadside to the current (Fig. 2)! Until you can see whether the outside is free from hazards, hug the inside shoreline. Only at very low eater should you deliberately seek the outside of the bend.

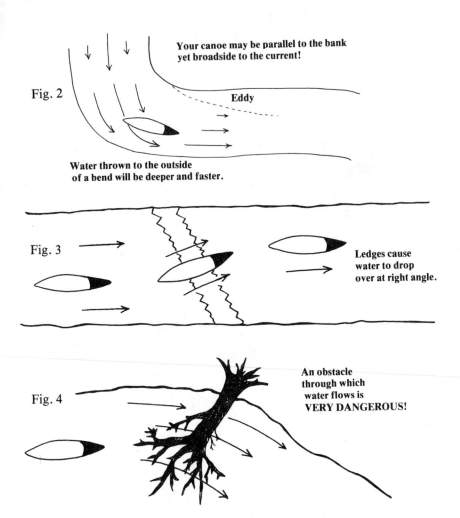

Fig. 2

Your canoe may be parallel to the bank yet broadside to the current!

Eddy

Water thrown to the outside of a bend will be deeper and faster.

Fig. 3

Ledges cause water to drop over at right angle.

Fig. 4

An obstacle through which water flows is VERY DANGEROUS!

Ledges that are diagonal to the shorelines will cause the current to drop over them at a right angle. This is another example where you may get into trouble if you are using the shoreline to judge the current direction (Fig. 3)

When moving water meets a solid ledge or rock it is turned aside; and that water cushion will also help to carry your canoe around. However, when the water goes through an obstacle, beware! The most common and most dangerous example is water flowing through the branches of a fallen tree. In paddling terms this is called a "sweeper" or "strainer" (Fig. 4). Watch for this on the outside of river bends, especially where the current has undercut the bank. If you do not want that 3,225-pound force pinning you on the branches, you had better paddle clear in advance.

Eddies are the extreme example of current differentials. They are formed when fast moving water is deflected around an obstacle, such as a rock. The

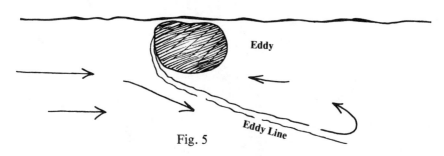

Fig. 5

void behind the rock is filled with still water or when the current is very strong, the eddy water will actually be flowing back upstream (Fig. 5)! The line formed by the current differential, where the main current rushes by and the eddy current is still or flowing upstream, is referred to as the "eddy line" or "eddy wall." An eddy may be a welcome resting place, but you must know how to cross a strong eddy line or you will be rudely dumped over.

READING ROCKS

Although rocks can be more damaging in swift water, they are also easier to locate. This is because they cause distinctive waves that reveal their hiding place. If the rock is close to the surface, the water follows the contour of the rock as it pours over and a raised convex wave appears on the surface (Fig. 6). This is called a pillow. Just remember that the pillows are stuffed with rocks. When greater volume of water flows over the rock, the following wave appears further downstream. You will need to train your eye to judge what rocks you can coast over without scraping.

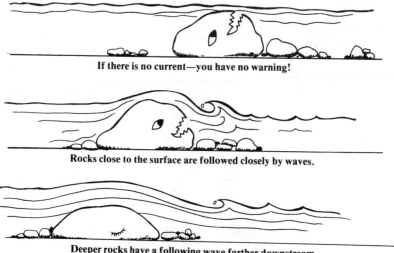

If there is no current—you have no warning!

Rocks close to the surface are followed closely by waves.

Deeper rocks have a following wave farther downstream.

Fig. 6

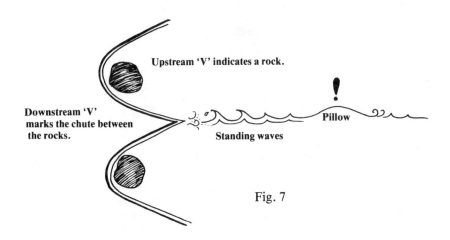

Upstream 'V' indicates a rock.

Downstream 'V' marks the chute between the rocks.

Standing waves

Pillow

Fig. 7

Current deflected around a rock will form a 'V' shaped disturbance called an upstream 'V'. A downstream 'V' is nothing more than the joining of two upstream 'V's; and so marks the course between two rocks (Fig. 7). The downstream 'V' often has a slick and glassy appearance. If it is followed by a set of standing waves this 'V' points out a runable chute. Beware of other signs of turmoil that indicate trouble!

It is the "standing waves" or "wave train" that mark deep water and can give the canoeist a wild, leaping ride. Like all river waves, these stand stationary while the water rushes through on its downstream course. They may be spotted by their characteristic orderly rows of pointed waves that decrease in size (Fig. 8). These waves are a vibration phenomenon associated with the dissipation of velocity energy when a shallow, fast current reaches a deeper, slower place in the river. Standing waves, therefore, mark deepening water, downstream of a clear path that lets the water through the rapid without dissipating its energy on the rocks. When choosing a route over ledges or through rocky rapids, look for long unbroken sets of standing waves. This route will lead you down the deepest, unobstructed channels. If the standing waves are big, you may choose to paddle alongside of them to avoid being swamped.

Set of Standing Waves in Orderly Rows Decreasing in Size

Fig. 8

Fig. 9

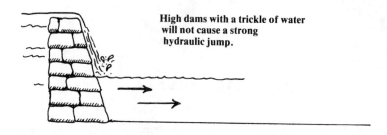

High dams with a trickle of water
will not cause a strong
hydraulic jump.

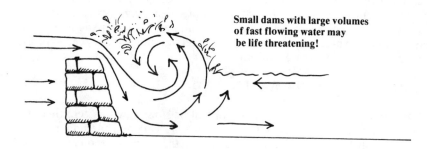

Small dams with large volumes
of fast flowing water may
be life threatening!

A dark line of water across the river followed by white foaming waves may be the only subtle warning you get that there is a drop ahead. When a powerful current drops steeply over a ledge, rock or dam it causes a hydraulic jump. This is what paddlers refer to as a "souse hole" or "hole." The force of the water drops to the bottom of the river, rushes along the bottom, then rises and rushes back upstream to fill the void (Fig. 9). Holes behind rocks make fun places to play. Dam and ledges that are strong "keepers" (holes without a side exit) are responsible for many fatal accidents! The keeping power of a hole is relative to the volume, speed, drop of the current, and the width of the hole.

THE RIVER IS YOUR BEST TEACHER

When you are scouting from shore, you may often see rocks that become quite invisible from your canoe. As you dodge past pillows and avoid suspicious waves, look back to see what caused them. This is the way to train your eye to see rocks and gain a feel for where the current is going and why. Soon rapids will lose their look of impassable chaos and become orderly. You can relax, thrill to the water's rush, and revel in the laughing waves.

Chapter 4

River Maneuvers

At the very heart of river canoeing are those dynamic tactics that use the current differentials and power of the river to enable you to perform effortless maneuvers. The steering tactic of lake canoeing is about as obvious as following your nose. The tactics of whitewater canoeing, however, are not as obvious: they are unexpected and sometimes even counter to instinct. A mastery of these maneuvers, from a full understanding to practiced skill, is the way to make rapids safe and fun.

STEERING IS FOR STILL WATER

Conventional steering has its place in still or slow water. Where there is plenty of room, the stern person does all the steering and the bow person needs only supply forward power. But, where the channel becomes narrow and winding there may not be room for the stern to swing wide enough to push the bow in a new direction. Then the bow person steers his end, drawing or prying as the overhanging poison ivy requires. As the current becomes swifter, though, this practice becomes increasingly hazardous. When

Fig. 1   **Steering is fine for flat water—**

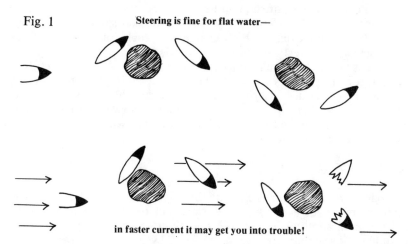

in faster current it may get you into trouble!

dodging rocks, for example, the canoe may not be headed the way it is pointed, but will be sliding sideways. Although the bow may be in a current going to one side of the rock, the stern could be in a current going to the other side (Fig. 1). A canoe sliding sideways, even slightly, makes a larger target for a rock. Whether a rock-strewn rapid becomes a cemetery or a "rock garden" depends on your knowledge and execution of the right maneuvers.

PARALLEL SIDE SLIP

The solution in slow-moving current is simply to side slip the canoe as you coast down at the same speed as the water. The bow person threads the nose of the canoe between the rocks and the stern person quickly moves the tail end over, keeping the canoe parallel to the current at all times. The bow person sees the rock first and makes the decision to go right or left. He draws or prys; the stern person counters with the opposite stroke—a pry for a draw and a draw for a pry, to move the stern in the same direction (Fig. 2). There is no need to shout. A frantic draw means a rock is dangerously close to his off side!

PARALLEL SIDE SLIP

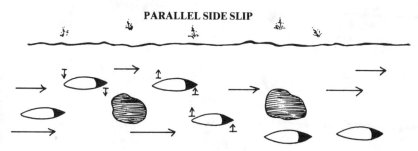

(Direction of paddle stroke is shown by small arrow.)

Fig. 2

We pointedly refute the often-published statement that a canoe must have forward motion for steerageway. In some cases it is far safer to coast at the same speed as the current than to charge into rocks or run the risk of swamping in large waves.

A canoe is not well streamlined to move sideways for long distances. Side slipping is for short dodges around obstacles. When it becomes necessary to move a long distance across a river against a fast current, you will not make it by side slipping. You will not make it by paddling forward either. Even by over steering, you will be swept broadside into what you wish to avoid. A back ferry is the maneuver to use.

BACK FERRY

The back ferry is one of the ultimate finesse maneuvers used in open boat paddling to move you across a current while back paddling. Here is how the back ferry comes into play: you are paddling down an exciting rapid when you suddenly see that the river is blocked by a sleeping dragon. You immediately jam on the brakes with a few back strokes, and the bow paddler sets a thirty-degree angle to the current with the stern toward the shore to which you wish to move. Keeping this angle while back paddling, the canoe neatly glides across the river (Fig. 3). (The thirty-degree angle is merely a good generalization. See Forward Ferry for a more in-depth explanation of why a ferry works and which angle to use.)

This, of course, looks simple on paper. Let us examine more closely the fine tuning of this elegant maneuver. First, contrary to popular belief, the bow person should set and control the angle of the canoe to the current.

Fig. 3   **BACK FERRY TO MOVE ACROSS SWIFT CURRENT**

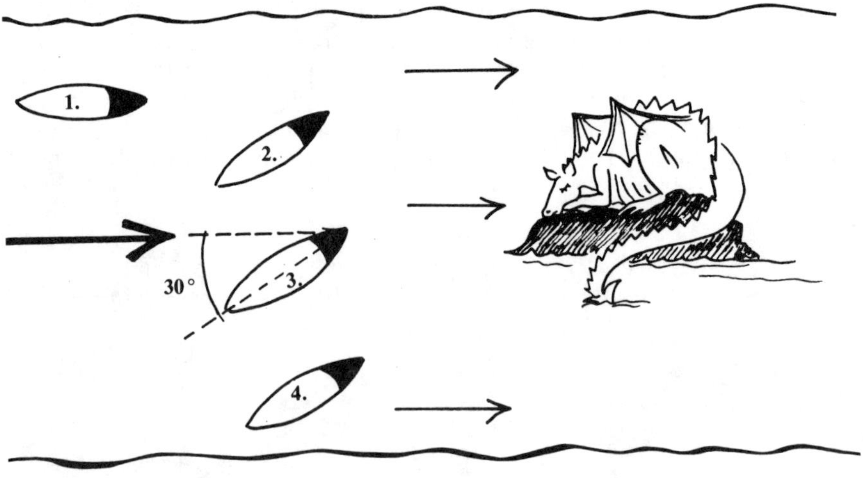

When you are paddling forward, the stern person is in a more effective correcting position; when back paddling (on flatwater—or against the current) the bow person is in a more effective position. If you are having difficulty feeling the angle of the canoe to the current, turn your upper body around. This is where that "compound back stroke" really does the trick. This stroke allows the bow person to make corrections in combination with keeping backward power. To draw: reach back and out. To pry: finish your back stroke with a quick pry off the bow (Fig. 4). The compound back stroke also prevents the stern person from doing sloppy back strokes that become reverse sweeps.

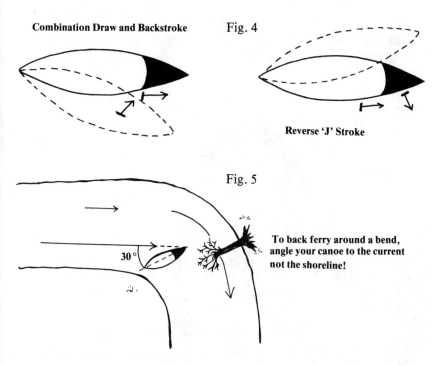

Combination Draw and Backstroke   Fig. 4

Reverse 'J' Stroke

Fig. 5

30°

To back ferry around a bend, angle your canoe to the current not the shoreline!

It is not easy to master both these correction strokes and a good feel for the appropriate back ferry angle. For this reason, when there is a need to perform numerous back ferries, it is preferable to have the more experienced paddler in the bow. Although it is more effective for the bow to set the angle in a back ferry, there is no law against the stern helping.

Now let us look at a couple of problems that often arise in moving through current differentials in back ferrying around bends and into eddies. To avoid a sweeper, a rock, or high standing waves on the outside of a bend it may be necessary to back ferry. The common mistake here is setting a thirty-degree angle to the shoreline instead of to the current. With the proper angle to the current the canoe may appear broadside to the shoreline (Fig. 5).

Back ferrying into an eddy may cause problems. All is fine as you slip across the river until you get to the eddy line. Here, where the water is deflected off the rock, the current is no longer parallel to shore. To adjust to this current differential you must increase your angle to break through the eddy line (Fig. 6).

TO BACK FERRY INTO AN EDDY

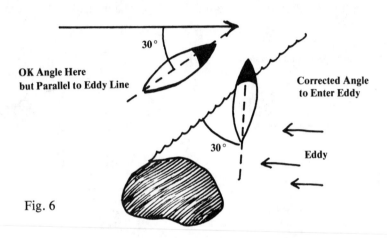

Fig. 6

The back ferry tactic is invaluable when maneuvering canoes with keels, or little rocker, and on wilderness trips where you may be running rapids with fully loaded boats. However, it is used less frequently with slalom boats. The extreme rocker of these canoes makes them harder to back paddle in a straight line; and, since they spin quickly, it is more common to turn them around and forward ferry instead.

Side slipping and back ferrying are more defensive-passive tactics. The maneuvers that follow all involve aggressive forward paddling.

FORWARD FERRY

The dynamics of the forward ferry are essentially the same as the back ferry, except this time you will be paddling forward, with the bow pointed thirty degrees toward the shore to which you wish to move. The downstream end, now the stern, will be correcting the angle (Fig. 7).

Moving through current differentials as you forward ferry from one eddy to another will add some thrills and spills (Fig. 8). The trick in getting out of an eddy is to build up enough speed to break through the eddy line quickly with a small angle to the current. If you are having trouble with the fast current swinging your bow downstream you will need to cross the eddy line with less angle to the current. Do not be fooled by the current deflecting off the rock. This current is not parallel to the main current.

Fig. 7

FORWARD FERRY TO MOVE ACROSS FAST CURRENT

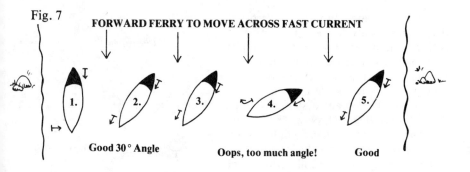

Good 30° Angle   Oops, too much angle!   Good

Fig. 8   **FORWARD FERRY FROM EDDY TO EDDY**

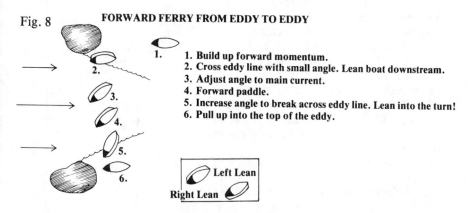

1. Build up forward momentum.
2. Cross eddy line with small angle. Lean boat downstream.
3. Adjust angle to main current.
4. Forward paddle.
5. Increase angle to break across eddy line. Lean into the turn!
6. Pull up into the top of the eddy.

Left Lean
Right Lean

Fig. 9   **HOLDING THE LEAN OF THE CANOE IS CRITICAL!**

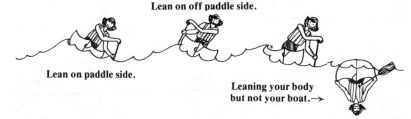

Lean on off paddle side.

Lean on paddle side.

Leaning your body
but not your boat. →

You will need to hold your canoe on a downstream lean from the time your bow hits the fast water until you reach the far eddy (Fig. 9). The stronger the current against your canoe the more you will need to lean. Reverse this lean when you enter the other eddy, as the water's force will now be on the opposite side of the canoe. Be ready to throw in a quick brace when you blast across an eddy line until you feel in balance with your partner and canoe.

Basically, a ferry involves two forces: the force of your paddling the canoe against the current and the force of the river current against the side of your canoe. Varying your paddling force and/or the angle to the current will determine your final direction of travel (Fig. 10).

What ferry angle moves you across the river with the least downstream slip? There is a trigonometric solution to find the optimal angle based on the ratio of your paddling speed to the river speed. For example, if your paddle force is equal to the current, the best angle is approximately thirty degrees (Fig. 11). Now if the current increases and you can paddle only one-half of the river speed, the ideal angle would be sixty degrees. (Fig. 12 illustrates canoe No. 1 with an angle of thirty degrees to the current while canoe No. 2 has increased its angle to sixty degrees. The vector calculations show that canoe No. 1 is further down the river bank than canoe No. 2) Paddling at one-fourth of the river speed means an ideal angle of seventy degrees. Therefore, contrary to what one might expect, as the current increases, you need to increase your angle for the least amount of downstream slip.

Understanding this theory on paper will help you evaluate your experience on the river. Because our canoes are not rigged with ferry angle calculators that take into account skill level and size of standing waves, you must learn through practice to judge what angle will be the most effective to get you to your desired destination.

EDDY TURNS

Eddies, those quiet pools behind rocks in a turbulent rapid, offer "rest and be thankful" places to wait for friends and to catch your breath. Some rivers lend themselves to being easily scouted from the boat by hopping from eddy to eddy. This of course necessitates that you master the skill to get in (eddy-in) and out (peel-out) of eddies.

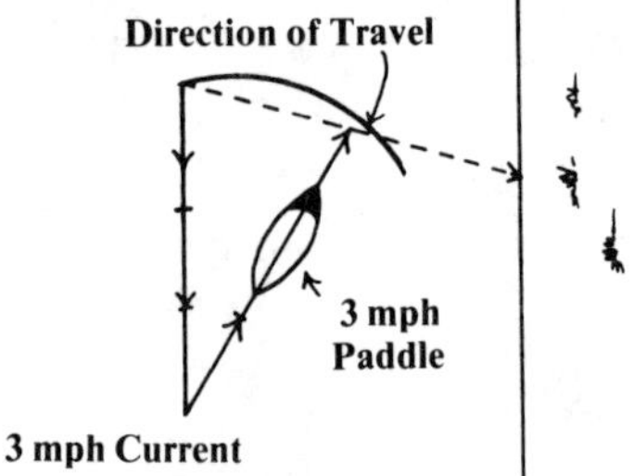

EDDY-IN

Drive into the eddy with forward momentum. At the moment your bow crosses the eddy line and catches the quiet water, your canoe will be spun

Fig. 10

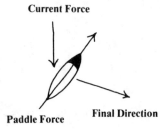

Fig. 11

Fig. 12

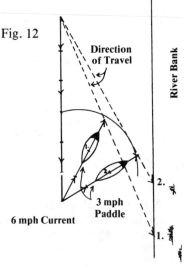

around by the onrushing river pushing your stern downstream (Fig. 13). Just as the boat initiates the spin you must *lean into the turn*. Experience and the river will teach you to anticipate the turning force that must be timed with the precise amount of lean.

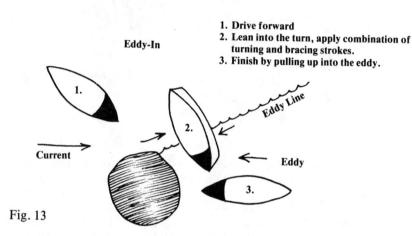

Eddy-In

1. Drive forward
2. Lean into the turn, apply combination of turning and bracing strokes.
3. Finish by pulling up into the eddy.

Fig. 13

Let us look closely at the precision needed to make this turn with style. First, your aim and entry angle are critical. You will get the most turning power out of the eddy current differentials if you drive across the eddy line at a right angle (Fig. 14). When paddling downstream into the eddy, the current may fail to spin you, and you will shoot right out the bottom. In driving the boat across the river, the stern person must keep aiming upstream of the eddy to compensate for the speed of the current. As many eddies are small, practice entering the eddy near the top, inches below the rock (Fig. 14).

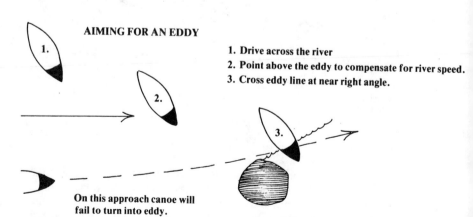

AIMING FOR AN EDDY

1. Drive across the river
2. Point above the eddy to compensate for river speed.
3. Cross eddy line at near right angle.

On this approach canoe will fail to turn into eddy.

Fig. 14

Fig. 15

Eddy-In

Lean into the turn!

A split second before the current differential begins to turn your canoe, apply your smooth blend of combined strokes. Suppose Douglas and Nancy are turning right into an eddy with Douglas in the bow paddling on his left. As they cross the eddy line, Douglas reaches forward to slice his paddle into the still water, holding a stationary pry. When the force against the paddle lessens he completes the pry and finishes with a strong forward stroke to pull the canoe up into the eddy. Nancy helps the turning momentum with a reverse sweep that ends in a low brace as she holds the lean of the canoe and then finishes with a forward stroke (Fig. 15).

Eddy-In

Lean into the turn!

Fig. 16

Let's try the same eddy turn with Douglas paddling on the right. This time he reaches out to grab the eddy with a stationary draw. Using this stroke as a high brace he leans the canoe into the turn. When the pulling force of the water against the paddle lessens he completes the draw and finishes with a forward stroke. Nancy allows him to lean the canoe to her off side while she brings the stern around with a couple of forward sweeps (Fig. 16).

Fig. 17

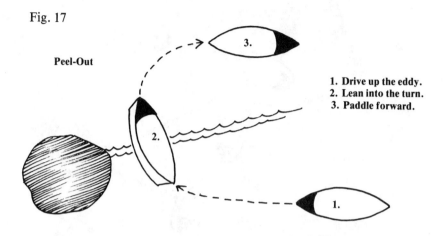

Peel-Out

1. Drive up the eddy.
2. Lean into the turn.
3. Paddle forward.

PEEL-OUT

The peel-out involves the same set of principals and sequences of strokes as coming into an eddy. Drive forward up the eddy and, as you cross the eddy line *lean into the turn,* applying your combination of turning, bracing and forward strokes (Fig. 17). It is important to build up enough speed to carry you through the eddy line and out into the main current rather than to ride down the unstable and turbulent eddy line. A peel-out requires a greater angle when crossing the eddy line than does a forward ferry so that the current catches the bow and spins it downstream.

REVERSE EDDY TURNS

Once you have mastered eddy turns, try doing reverse eddy-ins and reverse peel-outs. For a reverse eddy-in, while back paddling down the river, aim your stern into the top of an eddy and lean into the turn. For a reverse peel-out, build up backward momentum as you drive up the eddy, point your stern out into the current and lean into the turn. In both reverse eddy turns, use your combination of turning, bracing, and back paddling strokes just as the current differentials initiate the turn.

'S'-TURNS

Earlier in this chapter we explained that as the current increases you need to increase your ferrying angle. The 'S'-turn was developed on the basis of that theory. It helps project you across the river much faster and with the

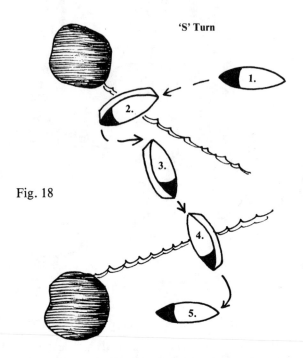

'S' Turn

Fig. 18

1. **Build up speed.**
2. **Break across the eddy line with more angle than a ferry, less angle than a peel out.**
3. **Keep paddling hard.**
4. **Eddy in—lean into the turn.**
5. **Pull up into the eddy.**

least amount of downstream slip. The difference between an 'S' turn and a forward ferry is that as you shoot out across the eddy line you deliberately allow the current to carry your bow downstream, so that you will be paddling broadside across the river. As you enter the far eddy, do not forget to reverse your lean and *lean into your turn* (Fig. 18).

SURFING WAVES

Surfing is a wonderful sensation. To catch the upstream face of a large standing wave, ferry out from a nearby eddy. As the bow coasts down into the trough, bring the canoe parallel to the current. If the wave is steep enough, gravity will hold you there as the current races by. It is a dizzy feeling (Fig. 19)!

If you use sloppy ruddering strokes (in which you drag the paddle against the current) to correct the angle, you will pull your canoe back off the wave.

Fig. 19

SURFING A STANDING WAVE

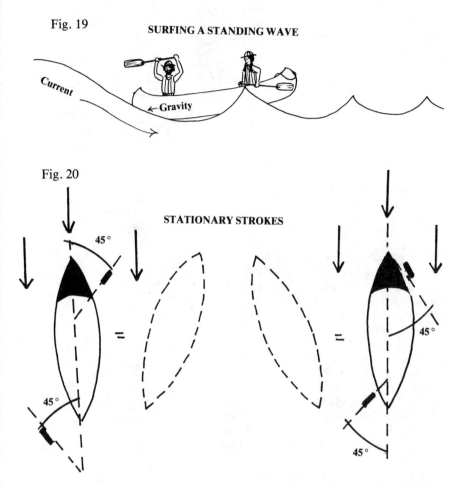

Fig. 20

STATIONARY STROKES

Holding paddle blade open to the current at a 45-degree angle will give you a stationary draw.

Holding paddle blade closed to the current at a 45-degree angle will give you a stationary pry.

This is where you can incorporate stationary strokes to make subtle corrections. Without lifting your paddle from the water you can change your blade angle to keep your canoe parallel to the current or to add just enough angle to ferry across the wave (Fig. 20).

PLAYING IN HOLES

You can surf a hole the same way you surf a standing wave. The upstream current caused by the hydraulic jump keeps you from being swept downstream (Fig. 21).

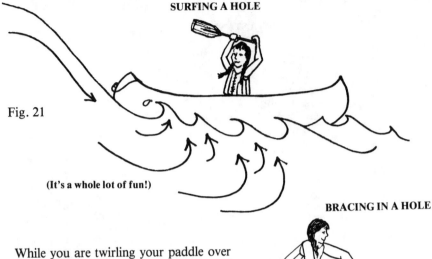

SURFING A HOLE

Fig. 21

(It's a whole lot of fun!)

BRACING IN A HOLE

Fig. 22

While you are twirling your paddle over your head, delighted in the sensation of being held by the power of the river, you may suddenly find yourself broadside! You can save yourself from a swim by quickly leaning the canoe and bracing downstream. Wow! What a great feeling . . . until your legs begin to cramp from holding the boat on a downstream lean. Now you might like to know how to get out.

If the hole is small, you will be able to pull yourself downstream by holding your paddle vertically (a high brace) and digging in deep enough to catch the downstream current. Another way is to paddle forward or backward out the sides of the hold. (Fig. 22).

Make sure you choose holes that are within your ability . . . avoid strong hydraulics, dams with no side exits, and large keeper holes that may chew up you and your boat.

PLAYING THE RIVER

Learning these river maneuvers from a book is difficult. It helps to be able to observe more advanced paddlers perform, flowing from one maneuver to another as they dance their way down the river. A competent team paddling together in perfect balance with each other and in harmony with the river is inspiring. To share this experience is even more thrilling!

Chapter 5

Rescuing Yourself and Others

The emphasis whitewater canoeists place on safety and rescues is in itself an admission of the potential hazards of the sport. Canoeing is fundamentally safe, but safety is a result of knowledge and good judgement. Paddlers who do not take the time to learn and practice basic skills may expose themselves to some of nature's most powerful forces or find themselves in situations that even experts would avoid.

No matter how good a whitewater paddler you are, when you push your ability, spills are inevitable. Capsizing in icy water may produce shock that numbs your brain and leaves you gasping for air. Swimming through turbulent rapids can be disorienting, and you will need to time your breaths between waves and holes. It is, therefore, important to practice the skills of rescuing yourself and others in rapids where the river is forgiving. This will prepare you so that when your canoe overturns unexpectedly, your reactions will be instinctive: "get to the upstream end of the canoe, feet up and downstream, look for a rescuer or a large eddy."

The first rule in rescues is to "never give up." Most canoes are lost not only because of an initial error, but because of failure to do the right things afterward. One must possess a knowledge of moves and consequences and a mastery of skills under difficulties. If you cannot muster power to go right, then make the best of the left. If you are in the worst part of the river and find yourself going backward, do a good job backward.

GETTING OFF ROCKS

If you come to a grinding halt in rushing water, you must act quickly. If it is not a first class emergency, it may be your only dress rehearsal for a first class emergency. When the canoe is lodged on a rock, the water rushes against it, rises up the side and pours in. The water pours in most easily when the canoe is broadside, but it will also pour in the stern when the boat is parallel to the current. When the water is shallow (below your knee) quickly jump out, *upstream*. Lift the upstream gunwale so the water cannot pour in. Pull the canoe off the rock and hold it in the current by the stern painter. While it hangs with the current, the bow person and then the stern person may climb back aboard. (It is important that you wear adequate protection on your feet.)

Suppose you are broadside against a large boulder in faster, deeper water. Quickly lean the canoe downstream toward the rock (which is contrary to one's instinctive reaction to lean away from danger) before the river climbs in and wraps the boulder with your canoe. The bow person should do a low brace and hold the lean, even shifting sides in order to brace downstream. It is the stern person who must now act. If it is too deep or too fast to jump upstream, the stern person can jump on the rock (Fig. 1). When the stern is

Fig. 1

Keep upstream gunwale up!

lightened or lifted, the current will catch the bow and carry it around the rock. If the stern person has remembered to grab the painter, she can pull the canoe back into the eddy below the rock and climb in. When the rock is awash and slippery, it is better that the stern person throw her weight forward so that the current can push harder on the weighted bow and pivot the canoe around the rock (Fig. 2). Of course, if the bow was closer to the rock the above would be reversed.

Sometimes the bow will slide up onto a rock, the canoe will stop, then swing stern downstream. The boat may slide free by itself or you can help push it free with your paddle. Do not get rattled because you are running rapids backward. Both of you should look downstream on your paddling side. When you spot a good eddy, forward ferry into it or do a reverse eddy turn.

Fig. 2

RESCUING YOURSELF

When you take in a lot of water and feel it sloshing about your knees, greater care is needed to prevent tipping over. Brace, backpaddle, and get into an eddy as soon as possible to bail. You have much better control of your destiny while upright and with your paddle in action. If the water completely fills the canoe, however, get out even though you could stay upright. The higher the canoe floats the less likely it is to pin on rocks.

Once over, hold on to your paddle and get to *the upstream end of your canoe!* Move hand over hand along the gunwale, or scramble right across the boat, but get there fast! Otherwise you could be crushed between your 3,225-pound canoe and a rock. Once you are upstream of your canoe, the safest position is to float on your back with your feet downstream and on the surface (Fig. 3). In this position you can see where you are going and

Fig. 3

Swim on back, feet first on surface.

you can push off of rocks with your feet. It is critical that you keep your feet on the surface; this is achieved by leaning back in your lifevest and doing a flutter kick. If you allow your feet to drop, the current differential will tumble you head first and your legs may be cut and bruised on the rocks. *Never attempt to stand up in fast moving current!* Even if the river is only thigh deep, if your foot becomes wedged between rocks, the water's force can hold you completely submerged (Fig. 4).

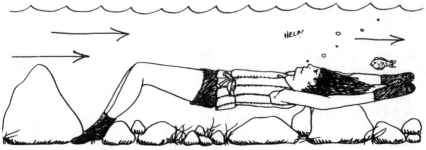

Fig. 4　　　**Never attempt to stand in fast water.**

Now, back to you and the canoe. You have scrambled upstream of your canoe and are on your back with your feet downstream. Where is your partner? Okay, your partner is headed for shore. Pull the painter free so that you can get away from the canoe, and keep the canoe parallel to the current. In this position the boat is less likely to wrap on rocks than if it is broadside. Once you are in a safe position and you have control of your boat, you will need to formulate a rescue plan. Is there a rescue boat on the way? Look for someone ready to throw you a rope. If not rescue is fast coming, ferry yourself into a large eddy by kicking hard and using your free arm. Once in still water, where you can get good footing, pull your canoe in or quickly snub the painter around a sturdy shrub.

In most cases your canoe will have a better chance of survival if you stay with it to keep it parallel to the current and tow it into an eddy. If, however, your canoe is dangerously out of control or the water is bitterly cold, abandon your canoe and strike out for shore as fast as possible to save yourself.

RESCUING OTHERS

Everyone wants to be a hero and rescue someone, but few will practice the skills in advance to be able to do it.

Many smaller rivers lend themselves to posting rope throwers before shooting difficult rapids. Throwers should be stationed below potential problem spots, on prominent points above large eddies. The old style throw ropes (sixty feet of coiled line) are no longer used because they are difficult to manage and can endanger swimmers in tangles of rope. We strongly recommend a "Throw-Line Rescue-Bag." They can be purchased through whitewater suppliers or easily made (see Appendix II). The beauty of this rescue-bag is that once the rope is stuffed into the bag it is always ready to throw. (Note: a rope must be stuffed in twelve inches at a time so that it does not tangle.) To throw, hold the end of the rope in your left hand and throw the bag underarm with your righthand. The weight of the bag will carry the rope out straight. The aim is all important. If your target is moving with the current, you must lead it ever so slightly. The rope should fall across the swimmer's chest (Fig. 5). If, however, your companion is on a rock, aim

Fig. 5

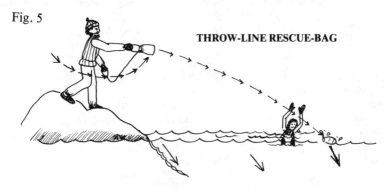

THROW-LINE RESCUE-BAG

just upstream so the current will take the rope to the rock. A little practice will improve your aim and teach you how far you can throw. If you miss, quickly put the end of the rope under your foot and hand-over-hand pile the rope at your feet, spaghetti style. (Be careful not to disturb this pile.) After you retrieve the bag scoop up some water and heave it again. Do not forget to grab the end of the rope!

When the swimmer takes hold and the river takes up the slack, there will be a tremendous pull. The rope can easily be ripped out of your hands or drag you into the river, unless a sitting hip belay is used (Fig. 6). Place the

Fig. 6

SITTING HIP BELAY

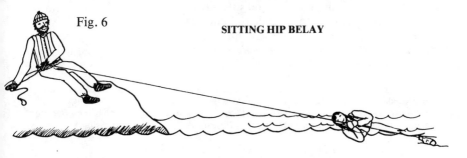

rope around your waist and sit down quickly where you can brace your feet. The hand holding the rope that comes around your body is the "brake hand." To stop the rope from running out, bring your brake hand across your stomach.

Rescues on wide rivers will often have to be done by a rescue canoe. As you charge down the rapid to save your friends, keep an eye out where you are going and formulate a rescue plan. Spin your canoe around above the swimmers, being careful not to run them over, and allow them to grab your stern painter. With a forward ferry, tow them to an eddy, asking them to help by kicking hard. In some circumstances it is better to have the victim climb aboard your canoe. You may choose to do this when the water is cold, the river wide, or the rapids shallow and rocky.

Sometimes the rescue is not complete when you get a victim ashore. The person may not be breathing or so weak from the cold as to be completely helpless. Basic knowledge of artificial respiration and hypothermia may make the difference between life and death.

Artificial Respiration*, called A.R., may be needed in certain river accidents. Remember to:

a. Open the airway by tilting the head back and lifting the neck;
b. Check for breathing: look, listen, feel;
c. If breathing is absent, start A.R.; maintain head tilt, pinch victim's nose, take a deep breath and form a good seal with your mouth around the victim's mouth. Exhale to inflate lungs, then remove your mouth to allow victim to exhale. Watch to see that the chest rises and falls. Repeat every five seconds, twelve times a minute, until he resumes spontaneous respiration.

Hypothermia is a lowering of the body's core temperature to a level where the body is losing heat faster than it can be produced and normal brain and muscle functions are impaired. To treat:

a. Remove immediately from cold water and protect from further heat loss. Take off wet clothes and protect from wind and cold temperatures.
b. If your victim is cold and slightly shivering, give him dry clothing and get him to produce more heat by running around, doing isometrics, eating high carbohydrate foods and drinking warm, sweet liquids.
c. If he is shivering violently and uncontrollably, has slurred speech, is confused, uncoordinated and stumbling, do not do the above! *Handle gently.* Rewarm by placing victim in a sleeping bag warmed by hot water bottles or other bodies. Start by rewarming the core and not the extremities.

---

*The procedures for artificial respiration and hypothermia are taken from *Emergency Medical Treatment,* a text for EMT-As and EMT-Intermediates, written by Dr. Nancy L. Caroline and published by Little, Brown and Company, Boston, 1982. (Used by permission.)

d. If your victim is not shivering, semi-unconscious or completely uncon-
scious, *handle very gently.* The slightest bump can be fatal! Insulate
from further heat loss and package him out immediately to the closest
hospital.

Fig. 7

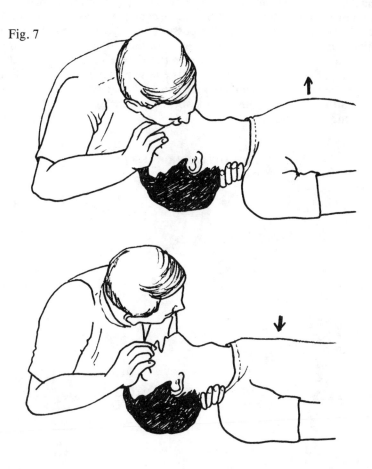

Although you may never have to treat a hypothermic victim or perform
A.R., it is strongly recommended that you take a first aid course. Rivers
often lead you far away from immediate medical help.

RESCUING CANOES

When the people are safe, think of how you will rescue their canoe. You
may be able to push the canoe into a nearby eddy with the bow of your boat.
Or you may choose to tie the upstream painter of the swamped canoe to

your back thwart and tow the canoe to shore. Be sure to tie the painter with a quick release knot so the capsized canoe will not drag you into danger.

If the river is wide, a canoe-over-canoe rescue is practical even in moderate current and waves. (Do not attempt this rescue in a rocky rapid because you may find yourself broadside against a rock.) The rescue canoe must be perpendicular to and upstream of the swamped canoe. The dumped paddlers move hand over hand to the ends of the rescue canoe, making sure that they are on the upstream side to avoid the possibility of getting crushed if the entire operation hits a rock. The bow person in the rescue canoe holds the boats perpendicular and braces downstream to help the stern person lift the end of the upset canoe over the gunwale. The bow person can also help lift the swamped canoe if the swimmers keep the canoes at right angles. After the canoe is lifted over the gunwale it is turned upside down and pulled up over the rescue boat (Fig. 8).

CANOE-OVER-CANOE RESCUE

Fig. 8

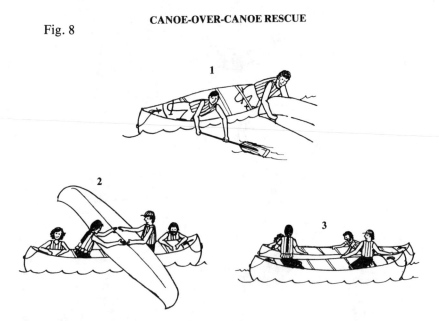

After the canoe is empty of water, it is turned right side up and slid back into the water on the upstream side. The easiest way for the swimmers to climb aboard is to bring their canoe alongside the rescue boat. While the rescuers hold the gunwales to steady the canoe, the wet paddlers can scramble in from the upstream side. This maneuver is a little easier said than done; practice it first.

Salvaging canoes pinned against rocks is not uncommon. Unless someone's life is in danger it is better to take time to formulate the best plan of action. Too often, a hasty action makes the situation worse. If the water is shallow, a line of people standing upstream of the pinned canoe may be able to lift the upstream gunwale and pull it off the rock. Getting folks out to the canoe may necessitate setting up a safety line. With your throw line tied to the canoe, secure the other end to a tree (Fig. 9).

Fig. 9

SAFETY LINE

If the canoe cannot be lifted off, it will help to add flotation to the swamped boat to displace as much water as possible. Try filling it with flotation from other boats or with dead wood. Then lift it again.

When the water is fast, it is better to sling your rope around the end of the canoe and pull from shore. (A strong pull may rip off painter rings, seats, and thwarts.) Try to move the end not fully submerged, the end most upstream or up in the air. Unless you have a large group you may not be able to pull it free without a mechanical advantage. Some groups carry a lightweight "come-a-long." You also can rig up a 'Z' drag with climbing pulleys and carabiners (Fig. 10). Use what you have available that best fits the situation.

Fig. 10

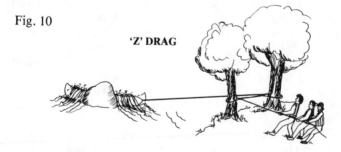

'Z' DRAG

When you salvage your canoe off the rock, it may be in need of some repair before it will float. An aluminum canoe can be pushed back into shape by putting it on a grassy or sandy spot and all standing in it. Tears and holes in most any kind of boat can be repaired with duct tape. If the boat is structurally damaged, you may need to do some fancy lashing or splinting. On long trips you may want to carry a fiberglass repair kit for your fiberglass boats.

You will learn more about rescues as you gain experience in whitewater canoeing. Spills are common, and so is the recovery of people and equipment; so the word "rescue" need not connote something unusual and dramatic.

Chapter 6

Strategy on the Hypothetical River

It is artificial to divide river canoeing into strokes, water reading, and maneuvers. In reality there is no separation of these skills for they are inextricably interwoven. This chapter will show you the integrated pattern. Let us call it strategy of whitewater canoeing.

With your fine equipment, your mastered strokes, and your practiced maneuvers, you are still only a chip on the water unless you can blend them all into a plan of action. We happen to be taking a trip down the Hypothetical River and if you care to join us, we would be pleased. This is no ordinary river: the Hypothetical River is at first a gently meandering stream with a few Class I rapids (see Appendix III). It becomes steeper; and as side streams add water, it becomes more and more powerful. The canyon at the end is rated Class IV.

At the put-in point, Edie, who is leading the trip, studies the river from the bridge. There is a riffle in sight, and she can see that the stream is neither in flood nor too shallow for the canoes. She has permission to park the cars in the clearing and informs us that canoes are best launched in the big eddy downstream of the bridge. Everyone is busy carrying canoes and gear down to the river and rigging the boats with flotation, bailers, and spare paddles. As the gear is sorted, Edie does an equipment safety check: Does everyone have a lifevest on? Are canoes safely rigged with adequate flotation and are painters secured? Who has the throw-line-bags? The first aid kit? Are glasses tied on? Mark and Dana will be "lead" boat and Edie's boat will be "sweep" (the last canoe). Edie establishes a running order and reminds us to space ourselves three to four canoe lengths apart.

You will paddle bow in my canoe. We put in, but wait in the eddy, making minor adjustment to knee straps. We review strokes to see how effectively we paddle together—right, left, back. Right and left seem confusing to us, so we settle on draw and pry. After a few more turns and braces, we push off into the gentle current.

At first the stream is narrow and rocky, so you are constantly drawing or prying to get the bow around obstacles. I do opposite strokes in the stern to thread the canoe through. We seem to paddle well together. The canoeing requires no words so we are discussing the greenness of the forest. It is so lush and dense that when we come to a fallen tree there is no chance of carrying around. We all wait our turn, and one at a time we bring our canoe in perpendicular to the trunk. We climb onto the log to lift the canoe up and over, being careful not to let the current swing it broadside.

The stream becomes wider and shallower. We come into a sweeping bend to the right. Typically, the outside bank is steep and wooded, the inside shore is flat gravel with scraggly alders. The lead canoe coasts into the bend letting the river decide its path. The current takes the canoe to the outside of the bend where the water is deepest. We drift along three feet from shore ducking under branches of overhanging trees. You reach for a branch to pull you over. I encourage you to use your paddle instead. The canoe ahead runs on a rock and swings broadside to block the only passage. We immediately start back paddling. After a few strokes I grab a branch directly behind me. Canoeing is full of exceptions.

A dark line of water across the river indicates there is a sharp drop ahead, so we back ferry into shore and get out to scout. We join the others who are looking at a three-foot drop over a ledge. When the group is together, Edie explains that if there were standing waves below she would not worry about running the drop, because if boats did spill they would be washed downstream and could be rescued without difficulty. Instead there is a large "hole" that extends across the river.

Our leader illustrates the back flow on the surface by throwing in a piece of wood. The log drops into the hole, pops up four feet downstream, floats back upriver and is tumbled in the trough for five minutes. Edie is afraid that with the forward momentum needed to plunge through the hole, the canoes may be swamped and be tumbled in the hole like the piece of wood. The only escape would be to swim out the ends or to dive down to catch the downriver current (Fig. 1). We all decide to carry our canoes around.

Fig. 1

Our next obstacle is a gravel bar. The lead canoe notes where the current runs through most strongly. Keeping their canoe parallel to the current, they side slip over to the biggest boulders, knowing the water is deepest beside them. Marc, in the bow, is using a cross draw instead of a pry for this shallow water. The fourth canoe cuts the corner only to get hung up on rocks. Unfortunately, canoe five follows them and has the same problem. Both teams must get their feet wet to wade their canoes over the gravel bar. Edie and Malcolm, who are sweep boat, wait until they are safely back on course before following.

After the forks we run a rock garden, about Class I +. You pick our course from the bow and I keep the stern in line with the current. The stern of one canoe whacks an obvious rock; the stern person had steered the bow clear but failed to account for the current. Ahead we see the white of waves, but the river narrows so there is ample depth. The lead canoe runs down the center, back paddling to help the bow rise over the waves. They back ferry into the eddy below where we all join one by one. The canoe that whacked the rock, however, overshoots the eddy. This team tried to set the angle from the stern which takes longer and requires much more effort. Luckily they make the next eddy where they wait for the other boats.

We paddle out the bottom of the eddy to the next set of rapids, a Class II, where we play follow the leader. Our lead canoe back ferries into a tiny eddy, inches from the rock, then pushes out to let the next boat come in. Marc and Dana proceed to ferry back and forth across the river, catching all the eddies they can, until they find a big eddy which will hold all six canoes. We do our best to follow their graceful maneuvers. This practice is appreciated when we see the ledges below. The first drop is runnable on the right, but the only place where standing waves mark a break in the lower ledge is on the far left. This rapid will challenge the precision of our back ferry. Edie suggests that the weakest teams portage and set up a rescue canoe and throw-line bags below the last chute. While waiting for the rescuers to get into position, we discuss our route and the back ferry angle needed. Marc and Dana run the rapid, making it look so effortless. Unfortunately, we are unable to make the left chute and capsize going over the lower ledge. After being towed to shore, we give an "all clear" paddle signal (see Appendix IV).

At Big 'S' rapid (Fig. 2), Edie anticipates trouble. The water has become more powerful, and she advises us to sneak close to shore along the inside of the bends. The lead boat heads out, hugging the left shore; but it is forced out by rocks at a couple of places and must back ferry into shore immediately after the obstacles. The second canoe gets out too far and is caught in the diagonal surface flow pushing them to the outside of the bend. When they see that a sweeper has fallen across half the river, they start back paddling frantically. Realizing they are on a collision course, the bow person increases the back ferry angle until the canoe is almost perpendicular to the shore (about parallel to the tree trunk). Luckily they back away; only the bow hits the top branches of the tree, spinning the canoe around. The canoe is now going backward and the paddlers forward ferry into the eddy where Marc and Dana are waiting. From this eddy, we all forward ferry across to the inside of the second bend and into the large eddy where we rendezvous.

Next we run through a small set of standing waves and eddy-out on the right to have lunch on the large flat rocks. This is an ideal lunch spot and a good place to play the rapids. We pull out the throw-line bags since many of us are keen to improve our throwing skill. As swimmers come through the chute with their lifevests on and feet downstream, we practice rescuing them. The weather is not what other people call swimming weather, but we are dressed for it—wool long johns or wet suits. After the swimmers have finished playing, two canoes go out to work on ferrying while the rest of us eat and talk.

Fig. 2

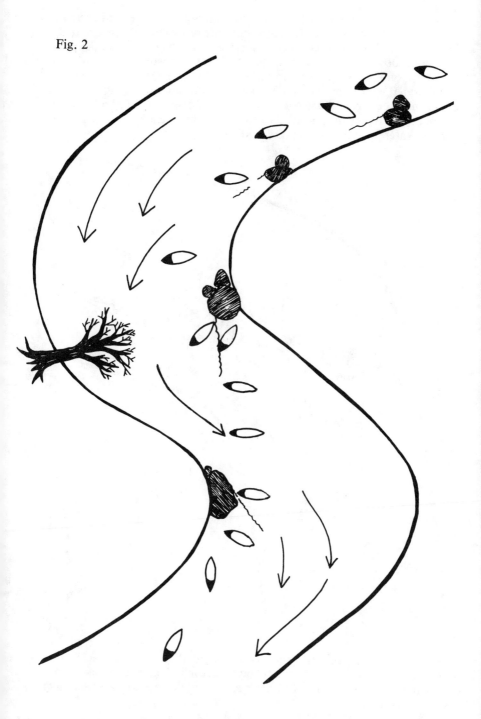

A young canoeist inquiries about flood waters on this river. Edie explains that at the start she studied the river from the bridge before she decided to launch there. If the water had been lower, she would have changed the put-in to a point downstream. If it had been in flood, she would have shifted to another river—unless we were in kayaks or decked canoes. The danger of flood water is swifter and more powerful currents—doubling the speed quadruples the force. These currents can sweep open canoes into big waves where they will take in water and capsize. Also most eddies are washed out and the water up in the trees makes landing and rescues dangerous.

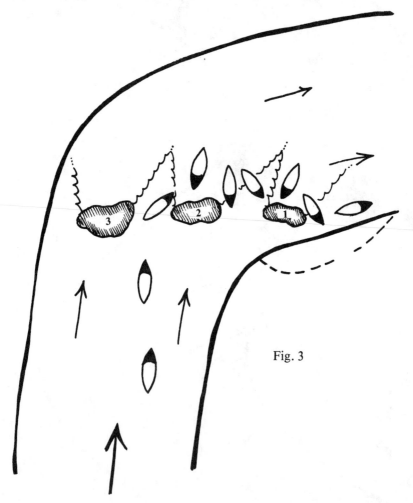

Fig. 3

After lunch we come to Three Island rapid (Fig. 3). The water flows between the islands, forming a rapid between each, then takes a sharp bend. At high water we would hug the inside shore and portage the large standing waves. At low water there would be no question that we would take the channel on the outside of the bend. Today the water level is moderate, so our lead boat selects the channel between the second and third island. They eddy-out behind the second island, forward ferry over to the first island, and then peel-out in the last jet of water. Everyone makes it; but a few boats need to bail.

We put ashore at the head of Imaginary Canyon, a Class IV section at high water. At this water level Edie rates it a Class III +. Our two weakest crews leave to shuttle the cars while we put the splash covers on the canoes. There is anticipation and excitement as equipment is made just right. We check the feel of our knee straps, try a few braces, and then the four boats peel-out in quick succession.

Edie and Malcolm are now lead boat with Marc and Dana sweep boat. The roar of the rapids is intensified by the canyon walls. There are enormous boulders with water pouring over them into deep holes that are followed by immense stopper waves. We guess which line of water passes clear and get into that current as far ahead as possible. Often we find ourselves charging across currents, running through waves sideways. Occasionally we must perform a quick back ferry to keep away from rock outcroppings along the cliffs on the outside of bends. Whenever we must plunge through large stopper waves, we dig our paddles in to pull the canoe through, always ready to throw a brace. After each difficult set of rapids, the lead canoe holds up in an eddy to see that everyone has come through okay. In the eddy, we catch our breath, and search the turbulent waters below for a safe route. Then we are off again peeling-out into the leaping waves.

As we plunge down the last wave train, the reflective serenity of the lake opens up before us. The thunder of the canyon recedes behind as we paddle onto the stillness of the lake. Half a mile across is the take-out where our friends are anxiously awaiting to hear of our adventures.

I have enjoyed paddling with you. Our team work through the canyon has been a splendid finale.

Chapter 7

Canoe Slalom and You

Slalom racing is a vital part of the whitewater sport. Its introduction from Europe in 1953 brought the whitewater groups together under the American Canoe Association and the independent American Whitewater Affiliation. Contacts with European paddlers added the concepts of eddy turns, paddle braces, and Eskimo rolls. Canoe slaloms developed and introduced these new techniques which revived interest in whitewater canoeing.

WHAT IS A SLALOM?

A canoe slalom is a preset course marked by pairs of poles, called gates, that are hung from wires over a section of river. Paddlers must negotiate these gates in order of their numbers, with the red pole on their left and the green pole on their right. This color coding indicates whether the gate is to be run upstream or downstream. Gates to be run in reverse are marked 'R.' A competitor's score is the total time from start to finish plus the penalties incurred on the course. Five seconds are added to your time for hitting a pole with your boat, paddle or body; ten seconds are added if both poles are hit and fifty seconds are added if the gate is missed completely, run in the wrong direction, or the body or bodies fail to pass between the poles. (Please note that slalom rules are changing nearly as fast as water levels.)

WHY A SLALOM FOR YOU?

Slaloms give you an opportunity to push your skill level in a safe environment, to meet and socialize with other paddlers, to buy and sell equipment, and to learn from observing better paddlers. Slaloms also allow you the freedom to challenge yourself on a course that simulates problems that you will encounter on rivers. For example: to make gate 7 (Fig. 1), you will have to drive high out of the eddy to quickly shoot across the river. This prepares you to handle the same problem safely on a river that has a five-foot ledge just below. On the slalom course, if you do not make gate 7, you have only missed a gate and can try again next time. On the river, you may have gone over the ledge.

A slalom is as competitive as you wish it to be. There will always be paddlers who are less skilled and those who are more skilled than you, unless you have just won the world championships. Set your own challenges. Your goal

Fig. 1

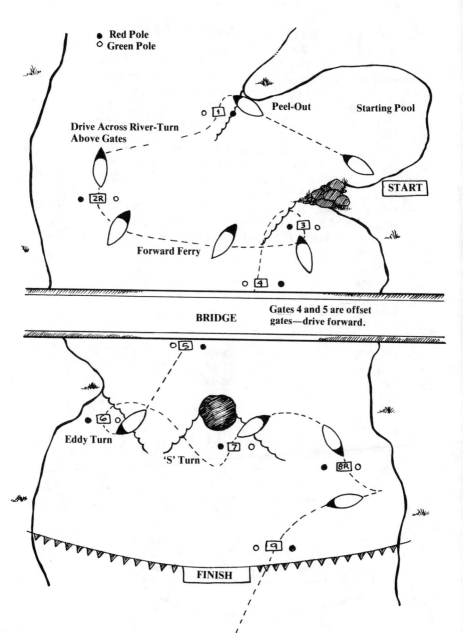

may be to finish right side up, to try for the gates you missed on your first run, to improve your previous time, or to have fun.

HOW TO GET STARTED IN SLALOM

Your first step is to find a slalom in your area. Go to your local canoe and camping store and ask about local races. Find out if there is a whitewater group and how to get in touch with members. You also may write to the slalom chairperson of the American Canoe Association who will send you an overwhelming list of races. (See references for the address.) Look for a race that fits your level of ability. Slaloms are rated C-D or A-B. A 'D' paddler is a beginner or novice; a 'C' paddler is intermediate to advanced; a 'B' paddler is an expert; and an 'A' paddler is skilled enough to try for the U.S. National Team. Reading over the race schedule, you will find both Slalom Races (SL) and Wildwater Races (WW).

Now you need to pick a class and enter. What class? OC-2M? C-2? K-1W? The first letter refers to the type of boat, i.e. canoe or kayak. The number is the number of paddlers: 1 is solo and 2 is tandem. The last letters are for sex: W is woman and M is mixed (man/woman). Larger races will offer Juniors (paddlers under seventeen) and Masters (paddlers over forty). Here are some examples of classes:

OC-1 means open canoe for one man.
OC-2M means open canoe, man/woman team.
K-1W means kayak for one woman.
C-2 means closed canoe for two men.

Approach your first slalom with confidence. Most races allow practice runs, so arrive early to take advantage of this learning opportunity. Get a good look at the course by walking the shoreline and you can decide at this

OPEN CANOES

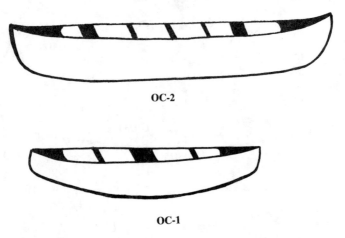

OC-2

OC-1

CLOSED CANOES

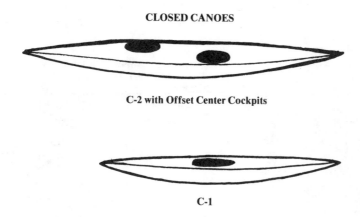

C-2 with Offset Center Cockpits

C-1

time how you will run each gate (Fig. 1). Rather than memorizing every gate (gate 3 upstream, 4 and 5 downstream, 6 and 7 upstream), visualize the sequence of maneuvers (up through gate 3, peel out and drive across to offset gates 4 and 5, eddy turn, up through gate 6 and S-turn to gate 7). Always be thinking two to three gates ahead. Slaloms often happen so fast that if you are looking around for gate 6, you may suddenly see gate 9 go by. After the course is closed to practice runs there is usually a competitors' meeting to assign gate judging stations.

Fig. 2

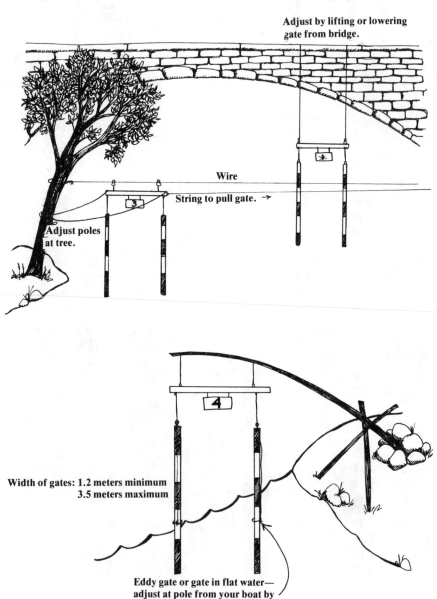

Adjust by lifting or lowering gate from bridge.

Wire

String to pull gate. →

Adjust poles at tree.

3

Width of gates: 1.2 meters minimum
3.5 meters maximum

4

Eddy gate or gate in flat water—
adjust at pole from your boat by
slipping loop up or down.

Here are a few tips:

—You usually get two runs in each class that you enter. The better score counts. Be a little more cautious on your first run so that you do complete the course. Go for the gusto on your second run!

—Remember to breathe. In the excitement, it is common to discover that you are holding your breath.

—As you slide through a gate, keep your paddle in the water to make precision adjustments. Doing an underwater recovery will minimize the chances of touching the poles.

—In backing through a reverse gate, both paddlers should be looking back on their paddling side.

—If you capsize, you are disqualified for that run and must leave the course. (Closed boats that are able to roll up may continue.)

—You may deliberately plan to omit a gate to minimize penalties or because it is too difficult for you at that time.

—When you have crossed the finish line you must stand by as a safety boat until three more boats have come through the course.

Now that you are ready for your first slalom, you may want to hang a few gates of your own to practice on flat or moving water. By far the easiest way is to hang three to four gates off either side of a bridge. Fig. 2 shows a few different ways to hang gates.

Slaloms are great places to learn and improve on skills for all levels of paddlers. Even if you do not feel inclined to participate, it is at races that you will see the newest innovative boat designs and the latest in paddling fashion. You also will have the opportunity to watch and compare the effectiveness of different paddling styles. If there is a race in your area, it would be worth your while to observe it.

Chapter 8

Wilderness Whitewater Canoeing

"Rapids are a challenge. Dangerous though they may be, no one who has known the canoe trails of the north does not love their thunder and the rush of them. No man who has portaged around whitewater, studied the swirls, the smooth slick sweeps, and the V's that point the way above the breaks has not wondered if he should try. Is there any suspense that quite compares with that moment of commitment when the canoe is taken by its unseen power? Rapids can be run in larger craft, but it is in a canoe that one really feels the river and the power of it.

SIGURD OLSON, THE SINGING WILDERNESS

The Allagash, the Moisie, the Winisk or maybe the Missinaibie? During the past winter months, a few of us were toying with the idea of paddling a wilderness river. After a beautiful afternoon of spring skiing, we gathered at Wayne's to discuss our interests and ideas about such an adventure. It was important for us, as it is for any group, to clarify our expectations, share our levels of abilities and question whether the four of us could form a compatible group. (Better now than a week into the trip.)

Jim was rusty on his whitewater skills but was keen on paddling a northern wilderness river. Wayne was attracted to a river that promised great fishing and superb scenery. Sally and I were enthusiastic about challenging a whitewater river and sharing the experience with two close friends.

We spread our maps of the eastern U.S. and Canada and started our search for a river that would fit our needs. The Allagash didn't seem to offer enough wild country. The Winisk was too expensive due to a long plane ride back from Hudson Bay. Although Sally and I had wanted to paddle the big water on the Moisie for many years, we felt it would be unfair to Jim and Wayne who weren't experienced whitewater paddlers. The Missinaibie looked good. The river offered 350 miles of boreal wilderness and a good progression of whitewater difficulty. Accessibility would be easy; we could drive to the put in and take the train back from Moosonee. The fact that the river had once been a major fur trading route on the Hudson Bay Company helped kindle a spark of adventure and romance. By late evening, we were commited to the Missinaibie Expedition and agreed on the time as the first three weeks in June.

Used by permission. Olson, Sigurd F. *The Singing Wilderness.* New York: Alfred A. Knopf, Inc., 1978.

I volunteered to buy, prepare, and pack the food; but first I wanted some menu suggestions. Sally said she would coordinate group equipment. That left logistics, maps, park, and river information to Jim and Wayne.

What about leadership? After a lengthy discussion, the two most obvious choices to us were leader-centered leadership or group-centered leadership. Since this group's combined whitewater and wilderness tripping experience was high, we opted for group-centered leadership. This meant that individuals would take on the role of facilitators to help process decisions. It would be important for everyone to voice his or her thoughts and opinions during this process and be ready to compromise for the benefit of the group. We also acknowledged that for emergency situations we would probably change to a leader-centered leadership model.

At dawn on June 3rd, we set off across Missinaibie Lake. After a detour to Fairy Point to see the Indian pictographs, we headed due north, leaving behind us the security and comfort of home. We were on our own now and this meant being able to handle any type of situation that would arise, whether it be a medical problem, and equipment breakdown, or a route finding decision.

Knowing that medical help might be weeks away, we carried *Medicine for Mountaineering* along with our expedition first aid kit. Most of us at some time had taken a lifesaving or first aid course. Jim and Sally also had taken an extensive wilderness E.M.T. (Emergency Medical Technician) course.

Our equipment was basic and its trail usefulness previously had been proven. We packed a minimum of gear (no folding camp chairs), yet enough to be comfortable (tents with no-see-um netting). We had come not to "conquer the wilderness" and try to shape it into our home; we came to be at home in the wilderness.

We ate lunch at the mouth of the river and by mid-afternoon we were scouting our first rapid, a straight run with big eddies on both sides. We found a scenic campsite halfway down the portage trail and decided to camp there so we could spend the rest of the afternoon playing in the rapid. It was a good way to start a long trip by playing: relaxing, and getting a feel for the river and adjusting to each other.

The relaxation ended the following afternoon when we arrived at Split Rock Falls, where we had a one-mile portage. After emptying the canoe, I secured the lifevests to the back thwart and placed the paddles in between the front thwart and bow seat. I then flipped the canoe up on my shoulders and headed down the portage trail. That left Jim with two packs. He hoisted the food pack on his back and threw the lighter equipment pack on top, resting it on the back of his neck.

Fig. 1

ONE-PERSON CANOE LIFT

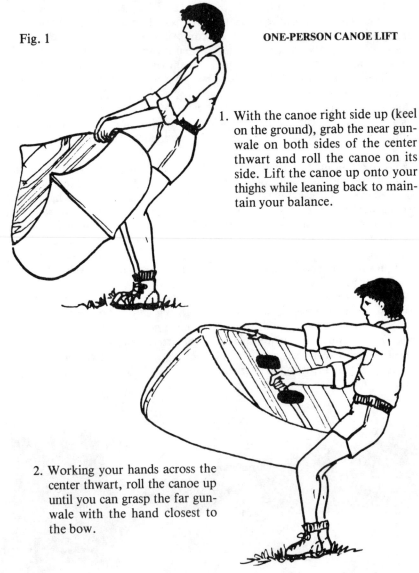

1. With the canoe right side up (keel on the ground), grab the near gunwale on both sides of the center thwart and roll the canoe on its side. Lift the canoe up onto your thighs while leaning back to maintain your balance.

2. Working your hands across the center thwart, roll the canoe up until you can grasp the far gunwale with the hand closest to the bow.

3. Slip your stern arm around the side, and with a one, two, three, roll the canoe up by throwing your whole body into the motion. As the canoe rotates up, duck your head into the yoke.

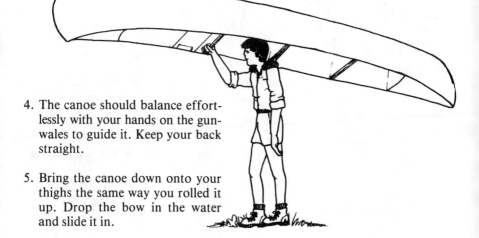

4. The canoe should balance effortlessly with your hands on the gunwales to guide it. Keep your back straight.

5. Bring the canoe down onto your thighs the same way you rolled it up. Drop the bow in the water and slide it in.

The easiest way for me to carry a canoe is by myself. I can balance better as I precariously negotiate slimy logs, hop from rock to rock, or climb over fallen trees. Getting the canoe up by myself is the hard part. Fig. 1 illustrates the traditional one-person canoe lift. An easier method, similar to the one-person lift, is to ask my partner for help. We both lift the bow onto our thighs and flip the front end of the canoe over our heads, leaving the stern on the ground. While my partner holds the bow up, I duck under the yoke. If I want help getting the canoe down, we do the same in reverse.

Halfway along the portage we stopped for lunch on a rock outcropping overlooking the roaring river. Wayne gathered wood to build a fire so we could cook some bannock. In order not to leave a fire scar, he removed the layer of top soil, set it aside and build a small twig fire directly on the mineral soil. After lunch, Wayne made certain the wood was completely burned; he poured water over the ashes and then replaced the layer of top soil.

The next few days were cold, windy and wet. It was a nice break from the blood-sucking bugs, but it also meant running rapids cautiously. If a canoe capsized it probably would mean setting up camp to treat the victims for hypothermia.

A few miles below Mattice we came to Rock Island rapid. We landed on the island, and after securing our canoes (it's most embarassing to have your canoe drift away without you), we scampered over the rocks to have a look. What a sight! Mountains of big standing waves, some four feet high, with a few unforgiving holes strategically located to make the route more difficult. Jim and Sally decided they were up to running this rapid. Recognizing the risk of swamping, they carried their packs around. Wayne and I chose to line this rapid and offered to be safety boat for them.

Although lining is physically less demanding than portaging, it can be more time-consuming and, if not done with finesse, can be dangerous. Remember, the canoe will be out there running whitewater without Wayne and me in the boat.

Where the water is shallow and the current tame, it is safe for Wayne and me to wade alongside our canoe guiding it through the deeper channels and lifting it over rocks when necessary. Holding on to the decks helps us keep our footing over slippery rocks. However, when the current becomes stronger, we pull out the painters and proceed to line from shore.

While I go ahead to scout the route, Wayne starts lining. Fig. 2 illustrates how he maneuvers the canoe around an obstacle:

1. Wayne pushes the canoe out into the current with a paddle or a kick. He sets a 30 degree angle by applying a slight pull on the bow painter and letting the stern painter run free. When the desired angle is obtained, he applies tension on both lines, and the canoe neatly ferries away from shore.

2. When the canoe has ferried far enough to clear the large rock, Wayne releases tension on the bow painter so the boat can swing parallel to the current. He then allows the canoe to coast down between the rocks by releasing tension on both lines.

3. Once the canoe has passed the rocks, Wayne pulls on the stern painter and the boat pendulums into the eddy.

Fig. 2

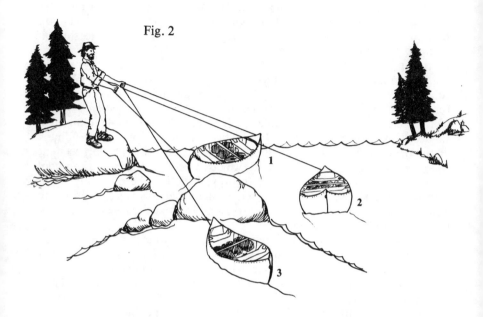

The next stretch of rapid and shore line is tricky and demands teamwork. I scamper out onto a large protruding rock to be in position to guide the canoe through some narrow chutes. Just when I am about to be entangled in the lines, Wayne throws me the painters and hurries down the shore. I maneuver the canoe through this section and then throw the painters back to Wayne. Well done! With my partner handling the bow painter and I the stern painter, we work our way to the bottom of the rapid. When we are in position to act as rescue boat for Sally and Jim, I hold my paddle up to signal them to come ahead.

When moving up or down the river, lining involves using the painters to ferry (or set) the canoe away from shore, around obstacles and back into shore. Remember, ferrying involves three things, two of which are controllable: (1) your paddling force against the current; and (2) the angle of the canoe to the current. (The third uncontrollable factor is the force of the current.) When lining, the paddling force (1) is replaced by the tension or pull you exert on the downstream painter and the angle of the ferry (2) is now controlled by working both painters. In Fig. 2 the canoe is simply doing a back ferry to clear the large rock.

Problems in lining arise when the canoe starts to gain too much ferry angle. In this situation, the downstream painter must be slackened. (In Fig. 2 this would be the bow painter.) All too often, in the excitement, the downstream painter is pulled harder which causes the current to build up on the side of the boat and water eventually pours in. Or, the upstream painter is let go altogether, and the canoe swings around, likely pinning on rocks.

Twenty-five-foot painters usually are adequate, although on a big river like the Missinaibie, we took fifty-foot painters. With short painters you may run out of line; and get pulled off balance or be foreced to stumble along to keep up with your canoe.

Studying our maps, we counted five contour lines crossing the river within the seven mile vicinity of Thunder House Falls and Hell's Gate. We calculated the river dropped at a rate of eighty feet per mile, which is very steep for an open canoe. During the first half mile, the river dropped only twenty feet. (A drop of fifty feet per mile or less usually is negotiable in an open canoe, depending on the skill of the paddlers, the water level, the steadiness of the drop, and the width of the river.) While scouting the top section, which was an easy Class II-III rapid, we discovered that there was no pool of water below the rapids to allow for miscalculations before being swept over Thunder House Falls. Even though the rapid was easier than many we'd run before, we all decided to carry. An old wooden cross on the bank was a reminder of the consequences.

We took a lay-over day at Thunder House Falls to explore the magic of the area. After this series of falls and canyons, the river dropped into the James Bay Lowlands and became wide and flat. James Bay was one hundred and fifty miles away. With tail winds and high spirits, we sailed our canoes, rigging sails with tent flies and log poles. Four days later we arrived in Moosonee, our take out point and the end of the expedition.

What is the magic that drew us to spend twenty-one days canoeing a wilderness river? How can we describe the thrill of plunging down a rapid, flowing with the power of natural forces; or the lonely call of a loon at sunset; the fulfilling taste of smoky pea soup after a long, hard day, the sharing of smiles around a warm campfire and of timeless friendships?

This you will have to discover for yourself. The door to the wilderness is opened by the spirit of adventure.

Chapter 9

Becoming a Whitewater Instructor

This chapter will not give you a prescription on how to teach whitewater canoeing. No two rivers offer the same teaching opportunities nor are any two groups at the same level of experience.

This chapter attempts to share theories and techniques that you may find useful while teaching: flatwater sessions to develop effective strokes; a progression for teaching whitewater canoeing skills; ideas for off-river workshops. These suggestions may help inspire your creative imagination and help you develop your own teaching style.

PUTTING STROKES AND FOLKS TOGETHER

The challenge in teaching whitewater is to balance knowledge, skill and experience with a varying range of student abilities, rivers available, and course length. Your work, as a teacher, will begin well before the course starts. You will need to familiarize yourself with the river you plan to use. Which section is better suited for an advance class or which rapid is condu-

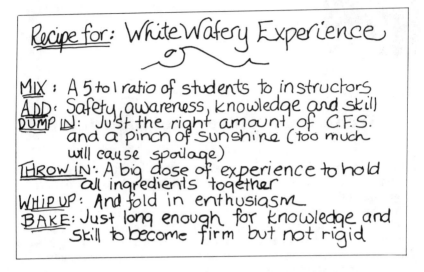

Recipe for: White Watery Experience

MIX : A 5 to 1 ratio of students to instructors
ADD: Safety, awareness, knowledge and skill
DUMP IN: Just the right amount of C.F.S.
   and a pinch of sunshine (too much
   will cause spoilage)
THROW IN: A big dose of experience to hold
   all ingredients together
WHIP UP: And fold in enthusiasm
BAKE: Just long enough for knowledge and
   skill to become firm but not rigid

cive to practicing back ferries? Write up a course plan which offers flexibility and provides plenty of time to practice and to play. If equipment is your responsibility, make sure it is ready to use. Are you mentally prepared to teach this class? Remember, accidents happen most often when one's mind is elsewhere; and students will quickly feel your lack of commitment and enthusiasm.

SETTING THE TONE

The tone an instructor sets within the first ten minutes is extremely important. A teacher needs to instill professional competence and a firm attitude toward safety. After taking care to learn everyone's name, start the class by introducing yourself and briefly outlining the plan for the day. This is also a good time to clarify expectations and put aside fears. When people are comfortable with expectations, they will be more receptive to what you have to teach them.

EQUIPMENT SAFETY CHECK

To avoid forgetting anything important, start your equipment safety check at the head and work down to the feet.

1. **Head:** helmets (if applicable). Check and adjust to fit properly.

Needs adjusting.

2. **Hats:** On cold days, see that people have wool hats. On sunny days, see that bald heads are covered with caps.

3. **Glasses:** Are they tied on?

4. **Body:** Are students adequately clothed for
   intense sun?
   swimming in cold water?
   chilly winds?

5. **Lifevests:** Do they fit properly? (Have everyone zip up vests and adjust straps.)

6. **Hands:** If it's cold, do students have mitts or poagies? (Rings and watches should stay behind.)

7. **Feet:** Does the foot gear protect the feet, is it reasonable to swim with, will it catch under canoe seats?

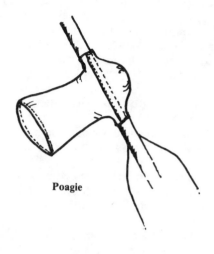

Poagie

Together with the students, check over the canoes. Are painters properly stowed? Do all the boats have adequate flotation? Are bailers and spare paddlers secured in each canoe? Are knee straps safely adjusted for unexpected exits?

As an instructor, safety is your responsibility! You may be held liable for any oversight. Make certain that your students have the proper equipment and have been instructed on how to use it safely.

If you plan to spend the first part of the day on flatwater, save the river safety guidelines until they can be more immediately applicable. Canoeing is not taught by talking at length about the history of canoes or the dynamics of tumblehome design. So, have your students pick up their paddles and put them into action.

MAKING YOUR FLATWATER SESSIONS FUN

Your flatwater sessions will depend on the time allotted, student enthusiam, and weather conditions. Do you have ten minutes for a quick stroke review, or are you organizing a two-day flatwater workshop? Is your group serious about perfecting precision strokes or are they a young group who are out for fun? Is it a warm day to practice rescues or is the wind blowing up whitecaps? The following are methods and games to inspire your imagination.

Keep it simple by keeping talking to a minimum and introducing only a few key strokes. It may be more appropriate to teach strokes before jumping in the canoes and getting blown across the lake. However, it is confusing for beginners paddling air to relate motion to effect. It may be preferable to have students practice the basic strokes kneeling along the side of a low dock.

In this way, they can feel the resistance of the water and the instructor can easily correct blade angles by placing a hand over the student's top hand.

A more exciting way to teach is by talking less and allowing students the freedom to explore and discover on their own. This is called experiential learning. Strokes taught this way would involve getting into the canoes right away, skipping the talk on land about canoes and strokes. To guide learning by students, offer challenges such as:

—Paddling on opposite sides, make the canoe spin 360 degrees to the right.
—Without changing sides, spin to the left.
—Paddle across the lake to the tall pines without switching sides.

Teaching experientially requires a great deal of patience on the part of the instructor. Students will often need support for taking the risk of making mistakes, so don't forget to give plenty of encouragement and positive feedback.

The number of strokes to be taught depends on the group's level of enthusiasm. Teach one or two strokes and then put them to use. After teaching the *Perfect Strokes* (forward, back, draw, pry), have the students play follow the leader through a course of slalom gates or milk jug buoys. After reviewing the 'J' stroke, go for a longer paddle and ask stern paddlers to do their steering corrections without missing a stroke.

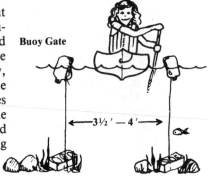

Buoy Gate

←—3½ ' — 4 '—→

GAMES

Games are an important tool in teaching any age. Often when the focus is on a game, the learning flows more spontaneously. Practicing strokes can be monotonous while playing challenging games enhances fine tuning of strokes. Water polo is a fun group game that will give learners a feel for their canoes. Try playing without paddles and using hands. If you have a series of slalom gates, buoys, or even sticks in the mud you can set up a flatwater slalom course. Let students invent their own sequence. To increase competition, give penalties for hitting markers or time students through the course. To decrease competition, keep switching partners.

Once students have a solid understanding of the basic strokes, introduce *Combination Strokes*, linking strokes together and fine tuning blade angles for efficiency. Playing with the English Gate is a challenging way to work on refining and blending strokes. The English Gate consists of one slalom gate (or set of buoys) around which a set of patterns are done (see Appendix V).

Dueling Partners is a suspense-filled way to introduce bracing. This is played by having one partner sitting on each end of the canoe, facing each

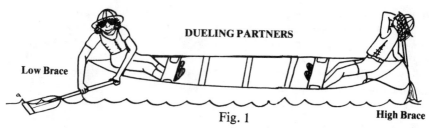

DUELING PARTNERS

Low Brace

High Brace

Fig. 1

other. (This makes the canoe very tippy!) Each attempts to throw the other off balance and save himself with a brace (Fig. 1). This game naturally leads into canoe rescues.

RESCUES

There are no set rules for good judgement; it comes from knowledge which is gained by experience. Because this is so true, it is important to give students firsthand experience with various kinds of rescues. In an emergency, this knowledge will help them choose the appropriate response. How should people be rescued? Should they rescue the boat by towing it to shore or do a canoe-over-canoe rescue?

Here are some rescue exercises for students to practice:

1. Dump the canoe and tow it to shore by a painter. (Students will quickly learn how much determined effort it takes.)
2. Time canoe-over-canoe rescues to see whether students can master the exercise in under ten minutes . . . three minutes . . . one minute.
3. Boat Over drill: first canoe rescues victims while the second goes for the upset boat.

On the river, speed may be a critical issue. Students need to learn, in various river situations, whether it is faster to tow victim and canoe to shore or pick up swimmers and perform a canoe-over-canoe rescue.

Staging a simulation of a river accident can be the most powerful learning experience short of the real thing. The more realistic the situation, the more seriously students will respond. Tell the group in advance that there will be a whitewater accident simulation sometime during the day. Ask them to respond as if it were a real situation.

Here is an example of a simulation which works well. The group paddles around a bend in the river to find a paddler on a rock with his partner (seemingly) crushed between the rock and the canoe. (Use a non-functional canoe.) The group may have to set up a 'Z' drag to remove the canoe, then treat the victim for respiratory arrest, hypothermia, shock or bleeding, and then form an evacuation plan. With large groups, you may wish to add more victims. It is important that you be realistic about what the group is capable of handling. When the students have done all they can, call a halt to the simulation and discuss what they have learned, what they did well, and what they would do differently next time. Many questions may arise; as a facilitator, you need to be up on your first aid knowledge.

Before students enthusiastically jump into the canoes and drift out of sight, do a final safety check. In the excitement of getting on the river, it is easy to forget to strap on a helmet or zip up a lifevest.

Prior to running the first rapid, it is important to heighten the students' safety awareness. When everyone's attention is focused, the instructor should review rescue procedures and clearly outline responsibilities. For instance,

Keep your feet up . . .
Get to the upstream end of your canoe . . .
If the paddle is lost, call "paddle" . . .
Never pass the instructor's lead boat . . .
The sweep canoe will always go last . . .
When you see a canoe dump, call "boat over" . . .
If you are not in a position to assist or lack the skill, wait in an eddy until the rescue is completed and rescue boats are back in position .

Since it is difficult to rescue two canoes, four people, and four paddles at once, stress the importance of self-rescues.

MOVING ONTO WHITEWATER

A good philosophy for teaching is: Introduce, Demonstrate, Practice, Critique.

"What I hear, I forget.
What I see, I remember.
What I do, I know."
OLD CHINESE PROVERB

Introduce: "What I hear, I forget." Introduce the process you are going to teach with a simple sentence which gives the name and a simple definition. For example, if you are teaching a forward ferry, a simple definition might be that it is used to move across a current to avoid being swept downstream. If you continue with information about entry angle, downstream lean, or angle of canoe to velocity of the current, the information will be lost. Students need a visual concept in which to plug information. This makes your demonstration critically important.

Demonstrate: "What I see, I remember." With a couple of precise strokes, demonstrate the forward ferry. It is important that your demonstration is done smoothly to set a standard of performance and to appear easy in order to boost students' confidence. After a couple of demonstrations, interspersed with pointers, invite students to try the forward ferry.

Practice: "What I do, I know." Encourage students with your enthusiasm and by participation to try again and again. Reassure students that making mistakes is a part of the learning process. Students also will follow the instructor's example.

Critique: Be sure to give honest, positive encouragement to even the timid eddy sitter, the clumsy over-they-go-again and the obnoxious watch-me kid.

Spend time with each individual, giving specific feedback on what they are doing well and how they can improve. There is a positive way to say just about anything.

WHAT TO TEACH WHERE

There are no set procedures as to what must be taught first; unfortunately, rapids on rivers are rarely in a good order of progressive difficulty. Ideally, the safest place to start beginners is at the bottom of a rapid with a large pool for rescues. When encountering a rapid that you have doubts about running safely with students, it is best to put ashore to scout. This may be a good opportunity to teach water reading and alternatives to running a rapid such as portaging or lining.

The river will dictate what to teach where. Where there is a consistent current without strong eddy lines, forward and back ferries can be taught. Big eddies with easily defined eddy lines are ideal for practicing eddy-ins, peel-outs and 'S'-turns. Big standing waves and holes are exciting places to surf. A rapid with a number of large rocks and eddies lends itself well to playing the river with a game of follow the leader. Big straight shoots, clear of rocks with a pool below, make great places to practice rescues. It is important to practice rescue skills in moving water! Be sure that you demonstrate self-rescue, use of throw-line bag, and ferrying a swamped canoe to shore.

OFF-RIVER WORKSHOPS

Seventy-five to ninety percent of teaching whitewater canoeing should take place on the water; yet, off-river workshops, either at lunch break or during the evening, are valuable to help assimilate theories and extend knowledge. An instructor should keep in mind that students will be tired after a long day of paddling. Sessions at night should be short, exciting, and inspiring. It is best to avoid talking about river dynamics, strokes, or maneuvers before students have been on the river. If you have an off-river class before paddling, equipment and clothing or the history of whitewater canoeing could be possible topics.

There are a number of topics and ways of presenting them that you might include in workshops.

Equipment and Clothing: This need not be a boring topic. Do a fashion show with Sunshine Suzy, Economic Ed and Wet Suit Wendy. Fill the room with a variety of equipment: wood, fiberglass and plastic paddles; examples of excellent and inferior models of helmets. Demonstrate adjustments on different styles of lifevests; bring a fully rigged whitewater canoe.

History of Whitewater Canoeing: This is obviously a challenging topic to make exciting. You may want to show a film about the Voyageurs, dig up old club movies of paddling in the fifties or put together a slide show on the evolution of the canoe—photographing drawings and pictures from books. Why not ask a canoeing instructor with long experience to come and talk about paddling in the old days?

DEMONSTRATION RIVER IN THE SAND

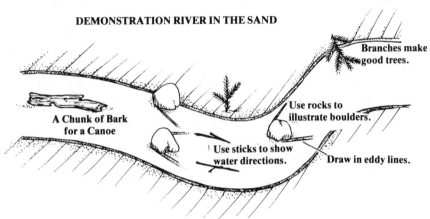

Branches make good trees.

A Chunk of Bark for a Canoe

Use rocks to illustrate boulders.

Use sticks to show water directions.

Draw in eddy lines.

Fig. 2

Water Reading and River Maneuvers: After lunch or in the evening are good times to explain in more detail the forces the current exerts on the canoe. For a visual aid, draw a river diagram in the sand. Use branches to represent sweepers, place a few rocks at appropriate places, draw in eddy lines and whittle a canoe out of a small piece of driftwood (Fig. 2).

To illustrate concepts when teaching indoors, use a blackboard or a flip chart. If you frequently teach canoeing groups, make a flannel board (see Appendix VI). These props can be used to replay certain river situations where students had difficulty during the day and, therefore, give a clearer understanding of why there were problems getting out of an eddy or why they dumped at 'S' rapids.

Films: Films or slide shows are a wonderful and easy way to entertain canoeists after dinner. They can provide an opportunity to watch some of the best paddlers perform. Seeing strokes and maneuvers done with precision puts the students' level of ability into perspective and inspires them to fine tune their paddling.

The American Canoe Association's Film Library has an extensive collection of whitewater films which they rent at a reasonable price (see References). In Canada, whitewater films can be obtained from the National Film Board. Check also with your local paddling clubs.

If you have access to a video, take the opportunity to film your students. It is a great way for students to see and critique themselves. On flatwater, film the English Gate sequence which demonstrates a blend of strokes. On moving water, it is best to film where a series of maneuvers can be performed.

Whitewater Safety: The film "The Uncalculated Risk," is a powerful introduction for an evening discussion on whitewater safety. If you organized a river accident simulation that afternoon or had any near misses during the day, now is the time to talk about it.

When teaching an advanced class on safety, read accounts of canoe accidents and diagram them on the flannel board. Analyzing what happened and how it could have been prevented helps heighten safety awareness.

Boat Building and Equipment Repair: After teaching on a rocky river, it may be necessary to spend half a day repairing equipment. Learning how to repair gear is an economical skill. This workshop might include: adding fiberglass or aluminum tips to paddles, banging out dents in aluminum canoes, replacing rivets, installing knee straps, and patching boats.

If you are involved with a summer camp, paddling club or a school outdoor program, your group may be interested in building canoes, making paddles, sewing paddling jackets, etc.

THE ART OF TEACHING

One of the rewards of teaching is seeing bright faces light up with discovered understanding. What students learn is a reflection of the quality of their experience. The more you teach, the more you learn about paddling, people, and yourself. When students have gained the skill and judgement to safely play the rapids without you, you will have fulfilled the goals of a whitewater instructor.

Appendix I

REINFORCING PADDLE BLADES

The life of your wooden paddle can be prolonged for many years by adding an aluminum or fiberglass tip to the blade.

For a metal tip: cut a strip of aluminum as shown below. Bend it over the bottom of the blade and fasten with rivets. Although an aluminum tip is easy to attach, it tends to catch on rocks.

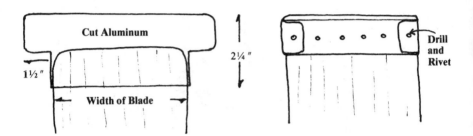

For a fiberglass tip: sand the bottom 6 inches of the blade, removing all the varnish. Glue cracks if necessary and pre-cut fiberglass cloth. When all is ready, paint resin on the blade and apply a 3-inch piece of cloth followed by a 6-inch piece. Wet out (saturate) each layer of cloth with resin as it is applied. Cover with plastic wrap, foam rubber, and plywood, and then turn paddle over. Now lay 1½-inch strips of cloth along edges until cloth is the same thickness as the blade. Finish with a 3-inch and 6-inch piece of fiberglass. Cover with plastic wrap, foam rubber, and plywood and clamp together. When the fiberglass has cured, unclamp; and, using a saber saw, trim off excess fiberglass leaving one-half inch on the bottom and one-eighth inch on the sides. Sand and coat with varnish or resin.

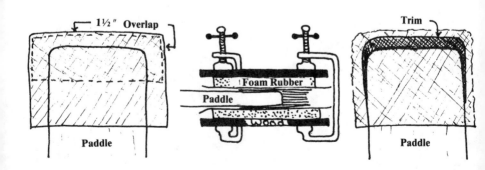

Appendix II

Materials:

65 feet of ½-inch polypropylene rope
48 inches of 1-inch nylon webbing for handle
30 inches of ¼-inch lacing
cord lock, 'D' ring and clip
6-inch diameter, 1-inch thick piece of ethifoam

Cut bag and bottom out of bright colored, heavy nylon material.

1. Sew the 15-inch edges together. Stop 1½ inch from top and back stitch.

2. Pin and sew bottom in.

3. Stitch webbing down the sides and across the bottom. Start sewing 4 inches down from the top (raw) edge. Reinforce at start and finish with

4. Turn top edge to inside ¼ inch and then ½ inch to form casing and sew.

5. Feed lacing through casing, attach cord, lock and knot ends.

6. Sew 'D' ring and clip (or velcro) to handle.

7. Make a ½-inch hole through bottom of bag, webbing and ethifoam. Candle the nylon.

8. Place ethifoam in bottom of bag. Feed rope through, tying one knot on the outside and one on the inside of bag.

9. Stuff rope into the bag, no more than 12 inches at a time to insure that it won't tangle when thrown.

10. Tie a hand loop at the end of the line and clip the loop through the handle so it won't get lost in the bag while in storage.

Appendix III

RIVER CLASSIFICATION

International Scale of River Difficulty:

CLASS I.   Moving water with a few riffles and small waves. Few or no obstructions.

CLASS II.   Easy rapids with waves up to 3 feet, and wide, clear channels that are obvious without scouting. Some maneuvering is required.

CLASS III.   Rapids with high, irregular waves often capable of swamping an open canoe. Narrow passages that often require complex maneuvering. May require scouting from shore.

CLASS IV.   Long, difficult rapids with constricted passages that often require precise maneuvering in very turbulent waters. Scouting from shore is often necessary, and conditions make rescue difficult. Generally not possible for open canoes. Boaters in covered canoes and kayaks should be able to Eskimo roll.

CLASS V.   Extremely difficult, long, and very violent rapids with highly congested routes which nearly always must be scouted from shore. Rescue conditions are difficult and there is significant hazard to life in event of a mishap. Ability to Eskimo roll is essential for kayaks and canoes.

CLASS VI.   Difficulties of Class V carried to the extreme of navigability. Nearly impossible and very dangerous. For teams of experts only, after close study and with all precautions taken.

(If rapids on a river generally fit into one of the above classifications, but the water temperature is below 50 degrees Fahrenheit, or the trip is an extended trip in a wilderness area, the river should be considered one class more difficult than normal.)

From the Safety Code of the American Whitewater Affiliation. Used with permission.

Appendix IV

UNIVERSAL RIVER SIGNALS

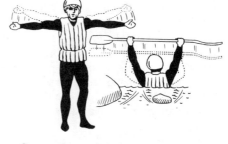

Help/Emergency: Assist the signaler as quickly as possible. Give three long blasts on a police whistle while waving a paddle, helmet or life vest over your head in a circular motion. If a whistle is not available, use the visual signal alone. A whistle is best carried on a lanyard attached to the shoulder of a life vest.

Stop: Potential hazard ahead. Wait for "all clear" signal before proceeding, or scout ahead. Form a horizontal bar with your paddle or outstretched arms. Move up and down to attract attention, using a pumping motion with paddle or flying motion with arms. Those seeing the signal should pass it back to others in the party.

All Clear: Come ahead. (In the absence of other directions, proceed down the center.) Form a vertical bar with your paddle or one arm held high above your head. Paddle blade should be turned flat for maximum visibility. To signal direction or preferred course through a rapid and around an obstruction, lower the previously vertical "all clear" by 45 degrees toward the side of the river with the preferred route. Never point toward the obstacle you wish to avoid.

Appendix V

THE ENGLISH GATE

The English Gate is an excellent training exercise. It consists of a set sequence of maneuvers done around a single slalom gate hung in still water (farm pond, lake or swimming pool). The exercise can be timed, starting when the bow of the boat enters the gate and finishing when the bow leaves the gate. A five-second penalty is added for each pole hit (see slalom rules, Chapter 7). Timing the exercise measures improvement of skill and allows comparison between techniques or boats.

To facilitate memorizing the sequence, it has been divided into four parts. Note that Parts II and IV are the reverse of each other, and that rolls, for closed canoes and kayaks, are done inward after passing the pole on the outside.

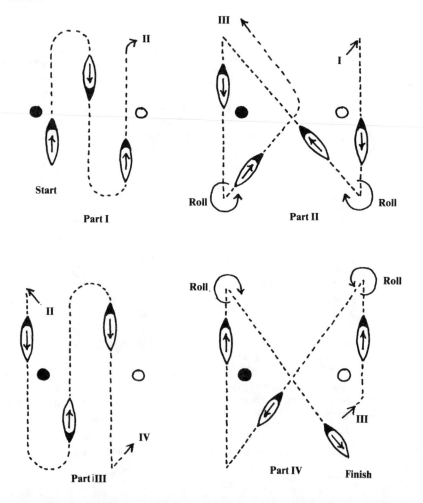

Appendix VI

FLANNEL BOARD

A flannel board, simulating a river, can be used as a teaching aid to review and explain in more detail river maneuvers, water reading, rescue procedures, slalom strategies or to diagram river accidents.

A good size board is made from a four-foot by six-foot piece of material with a flannel river sewed on. A straight section followed by an 'S' bend will be adequate for most any situation. From cardboard, cut out canoes, rocks, waves, 'Vs,' sweepers, current direction arrows and color them for visual contrast. To stick props to the flannel, cover the back with rubber cement or a prickly backing that can be purchased at a visual aids store.

To demonstrate maneuvers, make a canoe out of one-fourth inch wood, attach a stick or wire to it, and paint the bow black. Fix paddles with thumbtacks to help when discussing strokes used in various maneuvers.

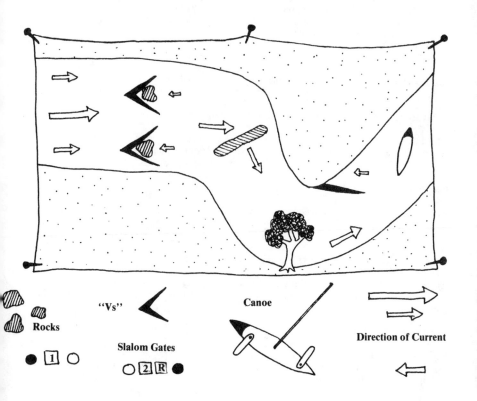

References

Books and Publications

The Complete Wilderness Paddler

By John Rugge and James West Davidson—A superb book for extended wilderness whitewater expeditions in open canoes. Covers techniques for flatwater and whitewater canoeing. Reads well with numerous black and white diagrams and illustrations.

RANDOM HOUSE, INC., NEW YORK, NY, 260PP.

Path of the Paddle

By Bill Mason—A complete and beautifully assembled book on canoeing, illustrated with black and white photographs and sketches. The author, a Canadian northwoods paddler, covers solo, tandem, lakes, whitewater, poling, portage, lining, safety and rescues.

VAN NOSTRAND REINHOLD, NEW YORK, NY, 192PP.

The Canoe and Whitewater

By C. E. S. Franks—A history of the evolution of canoeing and whitewater in North America from the days of the Voyageurs to canoeing today as a modern recreational sport.

UNIVERSITY OF TORONTO PRESS, TORONTO, ONTARIO, CANADA, 239PP.

Whitewater Racing

By John Burton and Eric Evans—A comprehensive guide to whitewater slalom and wildwater racing in closed canoes and kayaks for the beginning racer and the knowledgeable expert.

VAN NOSTRAND REINHOLD, NEW YORK, NY, 166PP.

The Best of the River Safety Task Force Newsletter 1976-1982

Edited by Charles Walbridge—This unique publication includes reports of fatal accidents and near misses with an emphasis on analyzing what can be learned from each incident.

THE AMERICAN CANOE ASSOCIATION, INC., LORTON, VA, 90PP.

Boatbuilder's Manual

By Charles Walbridge—An in-depth book on building fiberglass canoes and kayaks for whitewater paddling.

WILDWATER DESIGNS KITS, PENLLYN, PA, 103PP.

The Singing Wilderness, The Lonely Land, Reflections from the North Country

By Sigurd F. Olson—One of America's distinguished ecologists and conservationists, Olson writes of the harmony of the wilderness and sharpens our awareness of the beauty of the northern canoe country.

ALFRED A. KNOPF, NEW YORK, NY, 245PP.

The New Healthy Trail Food Book

By Dorcas S. Miller—This book is for those who prefer to prepare their own trail food. Dorcas explains in simple terms nutritional requirements, complementary proteins, and shares her creative, economical and tasty recipes.

THE EAST WOODS PRESS, CHARLOTTE, NC, 79PP.

Canoe

The magazine of the self-propelled water travel—Published six times a year. P.O. Box 10748, Des Moines, IA 50347.

American Whitewater

The journal of the American Whitewater Affiliation—Published six times a year. P.O. Box 1483, Hagerstown, MD 21740.

River Runner

Published six times a year. P.O. Box 2047, Vista, CA 92083.

Whitewater Schools

Nantahala Outdoor Center—Recognized as the finest center for whitewater instruction in the United States, NOC offers a wide variety of clinics for beginners, intermediates, advanced and expert paddlers in both kayaks and open and closed canoes. Their programs emphasize instruction in whitewater skills and safety procedures. Route 19W, Box 41, Bryson City, NC 28713.

Madawaska Kanu Camp—Certainly the best whitewater school in Canada, Madawaska offers weekend and week-long programs for the novice to expert paddler. The focus is mostly on kayaking, although they do offer canoe clinics. A major emphasis is placed on slalom gate work to help develop precision boating. 2 Tuna Court, Don Mills, Ontario, Canada M3A 3L1.

NorthWinds—Offers staff training and development workshops for clubs, summer camps, and outdoor programs. Emphasis is placed on skill improvement, safety and teaching whitewater. Also available for safety evaluations and as consultants in developing whitewater programs. Matty McNair and Paul Landry. P.O. Box 255, Madison, NH 03849 or P.O. Box 296, Smooth Rock Falls, Ontario, Canada P0L 2B0.

National Canoe Organizations

American Canoe Association—P.O. Box 248, Lorton, VA 22079.

American Whitewater Affiliation—146 North Brockway, Palatine, IL 60067.

Canadian Canoe Association—333 River Road, Vanier City, Ontario, Canada K1L 8B9.

Canadian Recreational Canoeing Association—P.O. Box 500, Hyde Park, Ontario, Canada N0M 1Z0.

Drawings: Dana Foster McNair
Photographs: McNair-Landry Collection